Jesus went to Nazareth, where he had been brought up. As was his custom, he attended the synagogue service on the sabbath day.

He stood up to read and was handed the scroll of the prophet Isaiah. He unrolled the scroll and found the place where it is written:

'The Spirit of the Lord is upon me.
He has anointed me
to bring good news to the poor,
to proclaim freedom . . . .'

Jesus then rolled up the scroll, gave it back to the assistant and sat down.

All eyes in the synagogue were fixed on him.

Luke 4,16-20

John Wijngaards was born in 1935. He studied in Holland and England, and joined St.Joseph's Missionary Society of Mill Hill. In 1959 he was ordained a Catholic priest. After completing a licentiate in Sacred Scripture and a doctorate in theology, he was appointed to the major seminary of Hyderabad in India. He set up *Amruthavani*, the Catholic communication centre of Andhra Pradesh, and has been involved in biblical apostolate world wide. Since 1976 he has lived and worked in London. In 1982 he founded the Christian resources centre *Housetop*.

John Wijngaards published a number of academic books on Scripture in the Netherlands, among them a major commentary on Deuteronomy. In the English language he is known for publications that combine scholarship and pastoral concern. Among them:

> *Communicating the Word of God* (Asian Trading)
> *Did Christ rule out women priests?* (McCrimmons)
> *Experiencing Jesus* (Ave Maria Press)
> *Inheriting the master's cloak* (Ave Maria Press)
> *The Gospel of John* (Michael Glazier)
> *The Spirit in John* (Michael Glazier)
> *The seven circles of prayer* (McCrimmons)
> —*Jesus for ever* (CTS)
> *God within us* (Collins)
> *For the sake of his people* (McCrimmons)

John Wijngaards

MY GALILEE
MY PEOPLE

Walking on Water

First published in Great Britain in 1990 as a **Walking on Water** book by Housetop (39 Homer Street, London W1H 1HL) and the Mission Book Service (St.Joseph's College, Mill Hill, London NW7 4JX).

ISBN 0 9507888 7 2

Artwork for cover by Jackie Clackson.
Cover lettering and design by Leigh Hurlock.
Illustrations by Jackie Clackson, Sheila Gosney and Alison Conti.
Printed and bound by Billings & Sons.

Welcome to this book

We, Christians, believe that, somehow or other, God the Creator has made himself known to us in a personal way.

That is what the Gospel, *Good News*, is all about.

God stands before us, face to face, in Jesus.

God speaks to us with words that we, human beings, can understand.

We believe that this is the meaning of *Incarnation*,
of God's Word becoming flesh,
of God, in some indescribable manner, living among us
as one of us.

This book has been designed to help you study this mystery from one particular angle, the human one. It is one thing to embrace a doctrine in global terms, quite another to explore its vast implications for our Christian life. I hope that the information I will provide and the reflections I offer, will stimulate your own further search, either by yourself or in a group.

I hope especially that this book will make you discover the Gospel anew. The Gospel is no dead letter that can be learnt by heart, - and then forgotten. The Gospel presents images of life that require constant re-interpretation in the light of the trials and challenges we meet on our way. True Gospel re-creates life.

It is important that you read the Gospel texts for yourself. The translations in this book are my own. If you do not as yet own your personal copy of the Bible, or if you possess one in an outdated turn of phrase, I recommend one of these two versions which combine accuracy of scholarship with readible style:

THE JERUSALEM BIBLE,
> Darton, Longman & Todd, London 1989.

THE GOOD NEWS BIBLE,
> The British Bible Society, London 1988.

The Second Vatican Council was a plenary meeting in Rome of the Roman Catholic Bishops of the world. It lasted from 1962 to 1965 and was attended by observers from all major Christian Churches. Its documents provide a statement of Christian faith within the reality of the twentieth-century world. I refer to its documents a number of times because they help us focus on what the Gospel must mean now. Standard publications of the text are:

W.M.ABBOTT, *The Documents of Vatican II*, Guild Press Paperback, New York 1966.

A.FLANNERY, *Vatican Council II*, Dominican Publications, Dublin 1975.

Housetop has produced a companion video to this book, of the same title: **My Galilee, My People**. It contains three half-hour instructional programmes (stories and illustrations) that supplement the material for this study. The video plus Guide costs (without VAT): £ 39.95, and is available from: Housetop Centre, 39 Homer Street, London W1H 1HL (telephone 071 402 9679).

I wish you a fruitful study. May the ever living words and images of the Gospel make you uncover 'things old and new'.

Table of Contents

page

GALILEE

I would like to take you, in a flight of imagination, to a village in the country side of Galilee. We enter a small hamlet, Cana. The year is 28 AD. 'We are going to watch a miracle', you think. Yes, we are; but it is not for making you taste water changed into wine that I am taking you with me. I want you to look at the scene with new eyes.

Jesus is standing on the dusty road between mud-walled houses. He has a small band of disciples with him, fishermen from Capernaum. Like the other wedding guests they have put on new clothes.[1] Mary, Jesus' mother who is also there, and other women, are holding oil lamps in their hands.[2] The sun is going down. The groom has gone to fetch the bride from her parents' home. We hear elated shouts. The procession has begun!

Jesus, who, we may assume, is related to the bride, shares everyone's excitement. There she comes, wearing a colourful gown, a crown of lace on her head, her face covered with a veil. People play on pipes and drums. There is singing and dancing to the music. The procession stops. The bride's father takes the veil from the girl's face and lays it on the shoulder of the bride-

---

1. Matthew 22,11-13.

2. Matthew 25,1-12.

9

groom, saying: 'The government shall be upon his shoulder'.[1]
Bride and groom look at each other. People clap and cheer.
Jesus too smiles at the bride and the groom when they catch his
eye.

What goes through his mind? We can be sure he is not thinking at this moment of the legal formality that sealed the marriage earlier that day. At that time the two families signed the
written contract, the *ketuba*, that spells out the financial security
the bride will receive in case of a divorce. Jesus does not agree
with divorce. He abhors the ease with which some scribes
condone it. 'What God has joined, no one should pull apart'.[2]
But at this moment he is not thinking of divorce. Like all the
other wedding guests, he allows himself to be transformed by
pure joy, the joy of these two people he knows, their happiness
in finding each other and starting a new family.

The procession arrives at the new house which the groom's
family have prepared for the young couple. There is no room
inside for the whole wedding party. A clearing nearby, a thresh-
ing floor perhaps, has been turned into an open air festival hall.
The catering is done in kitchens and backyards of relatives and
neighbours. Bride and bridegroom enter under the *chuppa*, a
canopy decorated with garlands and flowers. Bride and groom
exchange vows. They drink of the same cup of wine. Seven
blessings are spoken over them.

> 'Praise be to you, Lord our God, king of the
> universe! . . . .
>
> You have created joy and happiness,
> > bridegroom and bride,
> > rejoicing, song, pleasure and delight,

---

1. Isaiah 9,6.

2. Mk 10,2-12.

love and belonging,
peace and friendship . . . .
Praise be to you who give happiness to the bridegroom
and the bride!'[1]

Jesus' heart flows over with joy. When Jesus, later that night
or perhaps during the next day, changes water into wine, we
may easily be carried away by the religious implications of this
sign. Of course, the Eucharist is foreshadowed here - something
nobody present understood at the time. The Old Testament
Law, symbolised by the six jars 'meant for ritual washing'[2], gives
way to the new covenant, the banquet to which all nations of the
world will be invited.[3] But these wider implications of the sign
should not overshadow its immediate intent.

For Jesus is saying something about his people. Peasants who
eat and drink deserve no headlines in this world's press. Nor
can a shortage of wine after many generous helpings rank as a
major disaster. Yet, his mother's simple words 'They have no
wine', provoke an unheard of response. In effect Jesus provides
another 600 litres of wine[4] to the feasting farmers. It means the
continuation of the party; more dancing, more joy.

1. Scholars are unable to reconstruct all the details of a wedding
ceremony in Jesus' days. The outline sketched here is very
ancient. For a brief description and the text of the blessings, see
N.MANGEL, *Siddur Tehillat Hashem*, Brooklyn 1982, p.410.

2. John 2,6.

3. Isaiah 25,6-8.

4. The six jars held each 'two or three metrêtês' (John 2,6). A
metrêtê was equal to about 40 litres, or 9 gallons.

So often we focus on the sign in a one-sided way. We idolise the new wine ('You've kept the best wine until now!'), and dream of renewal, resurrection, spiritual transformation. But we overlook the other side of the coin, the reality that *is* changed. That is: we forget about the water. Without the limestone water of Cana, the earthenware jars, the kitchen boys, the blustering 'best man', the embarrassed groom and the revelling farmers, the sign means nothing.

In this book we will try to see the Gospel in a new light; from the other side, as it were, from Jesus' own experience as a Galilean. We shall see that the Gospel presupposes life rooted in everyday people and things.

To understand Jesus and his message we have to know the world to which he belonged. We have to know his people. None of us live in isolation. Neither did Jesus. Like us he imbibed his cultural outlook and his way of speaking and thinking from his family. Like us, Jesus became the person he was by responding to the pressures and challenges of society around him. Since he was a first-century Galilean, we cannot fully grasp his personality and his uniqueness without an appreciation of what Galilean society was like.

But that is not all. Jesus' devotion to his homeland conveys a message of its own. For devoted he was. Even though he occasionally moved out into other territories such as Phoenicia, the Decapolis, Samaria or Judea, he always remembered his special mission to Galilee.

> **'Land of Zebulun!**
> **Land of Naphtali!**
> **Way of the sea, far shore of the Jordan,**
> **Galilee of the nations!**

Your people, who live in darkness,
will see a great light.'
Matthew 4,14-16[1]

Yes, he died in Jerusalem. But after his resurrection he returned to Galilee. The women at the tomb were told: 'Tell the
disciples: 'He has been raised from the dead. He's no longer
here (in the tomb). He's going to Galilee ahead of you. There
you will see him!'.'[2]

There is much we can learn from studying Jesus' background.
It will explain traits of his character. It will put many of his
words in perspective. It will throw a new light on the Incarnation itself: if God wanted to become visible in one of us - 'Who
sees me, sees the Father'[3] - , why did he choose a God-forsak-
en place like Galilee?

'Study the Scriptures and you will see that no prophet
ever came from Galilee!'
John 7,52

The power of God's mysterious dealings with us overwhelms
us; all the more so the more we discover the human limitations of Jesus. Of course, we should have known. God's
Incarnation is *real* incarnation, that is: The Word God
speaks to us became human flesh and took on the limitations of our human living.[4].

---

1. Quoted from Isaiah 8,23 - 9,1.

2. Matthew 28,7; Mark 16,6-7; Luke 24,6.

3. John 14,9.

4. John 1,14: 'The Word became flesh and lived among us'.

ISRAEL BETWEEN THREE
CONTINENTS

*The 'land of the Jews', the country 'flowing with milk
and honey' which in Old Testament times became the
property of Israel, lay in between three continents:
Africa to the South, Europe to the North, Asia to the
East. On its western flank the land bordered the
Mediterranean Sea.*

Where on earth was Galilee?

Jesus lived in Galilee, two thousand years ago. At that time Galilee was a province of a country known by the Romans as 'the land of the Jews'. It makes sense to look at the whole country first; and for this we need to turn to a world map. There, in the part of the world we call the 'Middle East' today, we find its location: it covered roughly present-day Israel and Jordan.

Because of its central position it possessed valuable land and sea routes for international trade. It was the frequent scene of wars. All the great powers of the ancient world: Egypt, Hatti, Assyria, Babylon, Persia, Greece and Rome, occupied it at some time or other.

In the course of history it carried many names. The Assyrians called it *Mat Palastu*, 'hill country of the Philistines'; because of the Philistine settlements on the coast. The Greeks used the expression *Palestine Syria*, from which the English name 'Palestine' derives. The ancient Egyptians knew it as *Canaan*, a name we still find in the Bible.[1] Other biblical names were: *the land of Israel*[2] and *the Holy Land*.[3] This last name is still popular among Christians who consider it the 'Holy Land' mainly because Jesus lived there.

---

1. 'The land Canaan': Genesis 11,13; 13,12; 16,3; etc. Also 'land of the Amorites': Joshua 24,8; Amos 2,10.

2. 'The land of Israel' for the whole country: 1 Samuel 13,19; Ezekiel 12,19. Usually it denotes the northern kingdom.

3. 'The holy land': Zechariah 2,12; Wisdom 12,3; 2 Maccabees 1,7.

In Jesus' time, Palestine was divided into many provinces. Three of these provinces had a predominantly Jewish population: JUDEA, PEREA and GALILEE (see the map on the opposite page). The inhabitants of SAMARIA were the promiscuous offspring of Jews and Assyria immigrants. The IDUMEANS and NABATEANS in the South were Arabs. The people of the DECAPOLIS and the other Transjordan regions belonged to a mixed race with a hard core of Greek colonists. PHOENICIA in the North was inhabited by Tyrians, Sidonians and Syrians. Palestine was a true melting-pot of nations.

Luke, the evangelist, purposely fixes the beginning of Jesus' public ministry within a wider scale than Galilee, both in space and time.

It was the fifteenth year of Emperor Tiberius.
Pontius Pilate was governor of Judea.
Herod was tetrarch of Galilee.
His brother Philip was tetrarch of Iturea and Trachonitis.
Lysanias was tetrarch in Abilene.
Annas and Caiaphas were high-priests . . . .
Luke 3,1-2

History provides more details:
Tiberius was Roman Emperor from 14 to 37 AD.
His fifteenth year was 27/28 AD.
Pilate was the Roman governor of Judea, Samaria and Idumea from 26 to 36 AD.
Herod Antipas was tetrarch (king) of Galilee and Perea from 4 to 39 AD.
Philip ruled his kingdom from 4 to 34 AD.
Caiaphas was high priest in Jerusalem from 18 to 36 AD. His father-in-law, Annas, was head of the priestly family.

PALESTINE IN NEW TESTAMENT TIMES

NORTH

ABILENE

Sidon
Sarepta

MT LEBANON

SYRIA
Damascus

MT HERMON

Tyre

PHOENICIA

PANEAS
Caesarea Philippi

TRACHONITIS

Ptolemais

GALILEE
Capernaum
Magadan
Cana
Tiberias
Nazareth

GAULANITIS

BATANEA

SEA
of
GALILEE

AURANITIS

MEDITERRANEAN
SEA

Dora
Crocodilon

Caesarea

PLAIN
OF
ESDRAELON

DECAPOLIS

SAMARIA

R. JORDAN

Apollonia
Joppa
Lydda

Azotus

JUDEA

Emmaus

PEREA

Philadelphia

Ascalon

Jerusalem
Bethlehem

Marisa
Bethsura

Bethany
Quman

Esbus

Medeba

rippias

Gaza

Engaddi
Masaida

DEAD SEA

IDUMEA
Bersabe

Areopolis

NABATEA

Raphia

17

Luke presents Jesus' ministry within a wider historical setting, because he wants to underline Jesus' universal mission: 'all humankind will see God's salvation!'.[1] Is this to offset his earlier report: that God had sent Gabriel 'to a town in Galilee named Nazareth'?[2] After all, Galilee was a region of underdogs and nobody had ever heard of Nazareth! The tension between Jesus' humble origins and his meaning for the whole world is there for all to see.

The centre of the Jewish religion and Jewish power lay in Judea; in Jerusalem, in fact. The most flourishing 'modern' cities belonged to the Decapolis. Where did that leave Galilee?

Jesus' home ground

We can now have a closer look at Galilee itself. The main features of the province were its hills and mountains (see the relief map on the next page). The hills of Lower Galilee (around Nazareth) were not as high and rugged as those of Upper Galilee (around Safed and Gischala). Mount Meron in the north and Mount Tabor in the south stand out. Galilee possessed two plains: the Valley of Esdraelon on its southern border and the plain of Genesareth on the shore of the lake.

---

1. Luke 3,6; see also Isaiah 40,5.

2. Luke 1,16.

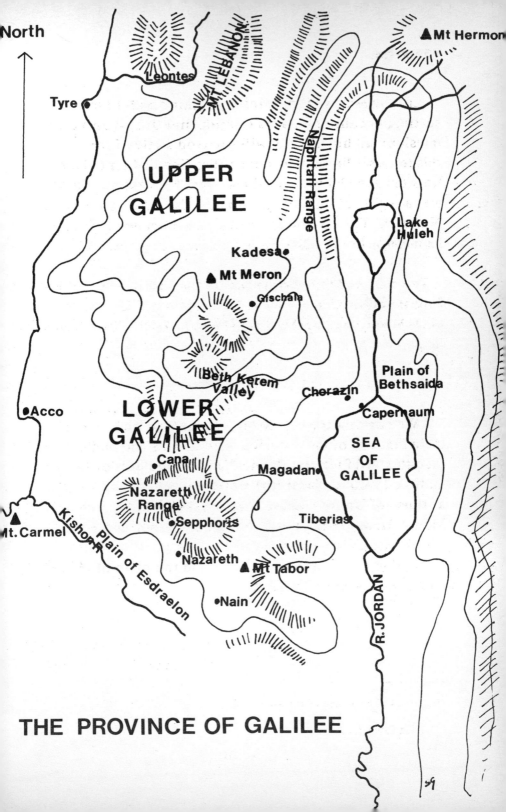

THE PROVINCE OF GALILEE

The name 'Galilee' is quite old; it may ante-date Israelite occupation.[1] It means 'circle' or 'region'. In the Hebrew Old Testament it occurs six times.[2] Isaiah gives the full name *Galilee of the nations*, which for Jews meant 'Galilee of the pagans'; the Greek book of Maccabees quotes the name with that meaning.[3] The name may well reflect the experience of the inhabitants of the hill country: that they were surrounded by other nations, pagans that is, on all sides.

Because of the valleys and low-lying lands on all its borders Galilee was vulnerable. Armies coming from the North or the South had easy access. They could march either along the shore, 'the way of the sea'[4], or along the Jordan valley.

Galilee in Jesus' time had three different kinds of towns and villages:
* **larger, Greek-style towns**; these were Sephphoris and Tiberias;
* **smaller Jewish townships**; among them we find Jotapata, Gischala, Capernaum and Corozain;
* **hamlets and villages**; Nazareth and Nain belonged to this category.

------

1. A.ALT, 'Die Herkunft des Namens Galiläa', *Kleine Schriften*, vol.2 , Munich 1959, pp. 363 - 435.

2. Joshua 20,7; 21,32; 1 Chronicles 7,76; 1 Kings 9,11; 2 Kings 15,29; and Isaiah 9,1.

3. Isaiah 9,1 and 1 Maccabees 5,15.

4. Matthew 4,15.

Jesus' Galilee was neither big nor famous. As long as people could remember, it had been a backwater, both in politics and religion. No illustrious kings had ruled here. No national prophet had been born on its soil. It possessed no monument of a great past. It was not even an independent country; it always was subservient to one power or an other.

For more than seven long centuries Galileans had been under foreign overlords. It is hard to imagine the impact this must have had on the native population. Always foreign soldiers on your soil who need to be billeted and fed; foreign officials who demand labour and a share of the crop; a foreign judge in court; foreign governors who import their own people and give them estates on your ancestral land. As a result, always being underdogs in your own country.

It had begun in 734 BC when the Assyrian king Tiglathpileser III captured Galilee. He deported many people to Assyria.[1] Historians believe these were the Jewish leaders and their families. The farmers and village folk were left behind, to provide the annual taxes.[2]

Assyrians ruled, Babylonians took over, then the Persians after them. Four hundred years with just one change of colonial officials after an other descending on Galilee. The Jewish exiles who returned home under King Cyrus of Persia,[3] seem to have settled mainly in Jerusalem and Judea. For the hill country of Galilee still had its rural Jewish population.

---

1. 2 Kings 15,29.

2. K.GALLING, 'Galiläa, Judäa und der Osten im Jahre 163 v.Christus', *Palästina Jahrbuch* 36 (1940) p. 64.

3. Ezra 8,1-14.

When Alexander the Great defeated the Persians and conquered Syria in 332 BC, the era of the Greeks began. Galilee, like the rest of Palestine, became subject to them. First the Ptolemaids predominated; they ruled from Alexandria in Egypt. Then the Seleucids who were resident in Antioch, got the upper hand. It was under these kings that the Greeks tried to impose their own religion on the Jews. A religious persecution was unleashed (167 - 164 BC) which also affected Galilee. It led to the Maccabean revolt.

The foreign masters of Galilee

734 – 539 BC. Assyrians, then Babylonians.
Galilee part of the Assyrian (later Babylonian) province of Megiddo.

539 – 333 BC. Persians.
Galilee part of the fifth Persian satrapy, 'Eber-ha-Nahar'.

333 – 120 BC. Greeks.
From 312 to 218 BC, Galilee a 'hyparchy' under Alexandria in Egypt.
From 218 to 120 BC, Galilee part of the 'eparchy' of Samaria, under Antioch in Syria.

120 – 63 BC. Hasmoneans.
Galilee a province administrated from Jerusalem.

63 BC – 70 AD (and later). ROMANS.
From 47 BC to 4 AD, Galilee part of the kingdom of the Idumean Herod the Great.
From 4 - 39 AD, Galilee part of the 'tetrarchy' of Herod's son, Herod Antipas.

Simon the Maccabee invaded Galilee in 164 BC and took some Jews back with him to Judea.[1] Historians say these were Jews living on the coast.[2] Again, the farmer population of lower and upper Galilee were left to their own devices. A period of intense confusion followed with civil war between Greek armies ravaging Galilee.

The Hasmonean John Hyrcanus liberated Galilee forty years later. Another sixty years of civil war followed, this time between Jewish factions. The Hasmoneans who were descended from the Maccabees, had made themselves high priests as well as kings. Therefore they were not accepted by traditional religious groupings such as the Pharisees.

Then the Romans entered the scene in 63 BC under General Pompey. In Jesus' time it was they who occupied the country, even if they partly exercised their power through middlemen such as Herod Antipas, Philip and Lysanias.

The influence of these foreign rulers had left their mark on Galilee. Each colonial power had imposed a network of its own officialdom: army officers, tax collectors, rural governors and traders who gradually became part of the population, especially in the main centres of government. Succeeding administrations introduced new languages. The foreign immigrants brought with them new artifacts and skills which the local people were made to copy. All this led to the emergence of a very cosmopolitan society in the trade centres of the Galilean plains.

---

1. 1 Maccabees 5,23.

2. S.KLEIN, *Galiläa vor der Makkabäerzeit bis 67*, Berlin 1928, pp.1-5; S.FREYNE, *Galilee from Alexander the Great to Hadrian*, Wilmington 1980, pp.37-39.

In the villages and small townships of the hill country, however, the original inhabitants tried to guard their Jewish origins. Although they had frequent contacts with the people in the plains, they sought to retain their own distinctiveness. Fear of the occupying armed forces, resistance to the foreign tax collectors, indignation at attempts to erode their faith and similar conflicts could not but harden their will to protect their identity.

No country like my country

With this new historical insight, we should, I believe, look at the wedding scene again. The first thing we notice is how *Jewish* the celebration is. Certainly, there are things that remind us of Galilee's cosmopolitan neighbours. The jars in the compound and the cups on the table carry a Cypriot design. The bride's dress had been dyed in a Phoenician workshop; perhaps in Tyre or Sidon. The master of the feast, the *architriklinos*[1], fulfils a role copied from hellenistic banquets. But the heart of the wedding, the main rituals, its philosophy, the cultural and religious values it enshrines, are a hundred per cent Jewish. It fills us with admiration for these simple country folk who kept their precious traditions intact in spite of so many eroding influences.

Secondly, we understand better now the almost fanatical love these people bore towards their own country. We cherish a possession all the more if we are in danger of losing it. The

------

1. The term literally means 'head of the three tables'. According to Greek custom, tables were arranged in a horseshoe for banquets. The person in charge of the feast looked after food and drink, seating arrangements, and so on. The function is alluded to in Sirach 32,1-2.

Treading the grapes was a joyful activity at the end of the harvest. 'The days are coming when harvest will follow ploughing, the treading of grapes the sowing. Then the mountains will run with new wine. All the hills will flow with it' (Amos 9,13).

Galileans loved their land, their religious heritage, that tiny part of the world that was their own. Jesus was one of them. He, too, loved his Galilee.

Jesus' love for his country was too rich and too deep to exclude other people in a narrow-minded nationalism, as we will see in the following chapters. His love for Galilee was nonetheless real. We cannot truly love the world at large and all people universally, if we do not begin by loving our own part of the world and its inhabitants in a special way.

The Telugus in India have an interesting song which expresses a deep human reality.

> 'Of all villages in the land
>   my own village is dearest to me.
> Of all streets in my village
>   my own street is dearest to me.
> Of all homes in my street
>   my own home is dearest to me.'

Unless we are anchored in our own home, our own street, our own village and our own country, we cannot reach out to other people and understand how they too have *their* Galilee, which paradoxically, is as dear to them as our own is to us.

Every person's Galilee is unique. Jesus' 'kingdom of heaven' does not float in the air; it rests on every individual, human piece of soil. The new wine he presents is not created out of nothing; it is a transformation of the plain water found in the kitchens of everyday life.

And that is only the beginning of the mystery of Galilee.

QUESTIONS FOR PERSONAL STUDY

1. Jesus loved Galilee and Galileans. Others did not. They looked down on Galilee.

> **'Study the Scriptures and you will see that no prophet ever came from Galilee!'** (Read John 7,52).

What are the implications of this fact for you?

2. In all four Gospels we are told Jesus returned to Galilee after his resurrection.

> **'He is going to Galilee ahead of you. There you will see him!'** (Read Matthew 28,7; Mark 16,6-7; Luke 24,6; John 21,1-14).

Was it important for Jesus to visit Galilee once more?
Why?

3. Comment on this passage of Vatican II in the light of your realisation that Jesus was a Galilean:

> **He who is 'the image of the invisible God' (Colossians 1,15) is himself the perfect human being . . . . By his incarnation the Son of God has united himself in some way with every human person. He worked with human hands. He thought with a human mind. He acted with a human will and loved with a human heart. Born of the Virgin Mary he has truly been made one of us, like us in all things except sin.'**

> *The Church in the Modern World*, no 22.

Space for your own notes.

CAPERNAUM

When Jesus was baptised by John the Baptist, he received a vision from his Father.[1] He knew that the Father was now sending him to call people to repentance and to preach his kingdom of love. How was he to achieve this difficult task?

Jesus needed time to think. That is why he went into the desert. He made a retreat of forty days to prepare himself. What was his approach to be like? Should he present himself as a general or a politician? The temptation story tells us the outcome of his prayerful reflection. He realised that his Father did not want him to rely on the secular means of money, power and fame.[2] God's kingdom of love can only be spread by love . . . .

On the other hand, Jesus also knew that he had to be practical; that he needed to use his common sense. Later we hear him tell his apostles to be simple as doves, yet clever as snakes.[3] And he also believed in planning: a man building a tower should get his sums right first; a king should plan his strategy before going

---

1. Matthew 3,13-17.

2. Matthew 4,1-11; about the meaning of the temptation story, see J.WIJNGAARDS, *Jesus for Ever*, London 1988, pp. 60 - 64.

3. Matthew 10,16.

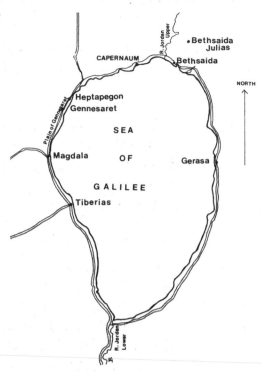

The sixth-century writer Theodosius describes the traditional places for Christian pilgrims:
'From Tiberias to Magdala, where the Lady Mary was born, two miles.
From Magdala to Seven Fountains (= Ayn Tabgha), where the Lord Christ baptised the apostles, is two miles. There he also fed the crowd with five loaves and two fishes.
From Seven Fountains to Capernaum two miles.
From Capernaum to Bethsaida, where the Apostles Peter, Andrew, Philip and the sons of Zebedee were born, two miles.'[1]

---

1. *Itinerarium Hierosolymitanum*, Vienna 1898, pp. 137-138. The Roman mile was 1.48 km. The distances are not correct.

to war.[1] Jesus recognised that he could not change the world on his own. He needed to find allies - and the right place to work from . . . .

We have already seen that Galilee consisted roughly of two areas: the hill country and the plains. To reach out to the whole province, he needed to put his centre in the plains; preferably in the pivotal plain north of the lake. There everything came together: government, trade, religious leadership. From there, like spokes from a hub, roads ran to the valleys and hills, and even to the neighbouring provinces. There, too, he would find the people who could help him in his work.

Tiberias, west of the lake, was the actual capital. Herod Antipas resided there. Much of Galilee's wealth and political power was concentrated in that city. But Jesus rejected it as a centre for his ministry. The reasons are not difficult to understand. Tiberias had been built by Herod Antipas in 13 AD as a totally *Greek* city. It possessed a stadium for horse races, public baths for the rich, a luxurious palace and a hall for the city council.

Even though Jews too lived there, it was considered a monument of foreign imposition. Herod, himself an Idumean, dedicated the city to the Roman Emperor, Tiberius. Moreover, overriding Jewish sensitivities he had built the centre of the city on an old cemetery, thus desecrating the tombs and making the whole city 'unclean'. Flavius Josephus, a historian of Jesus' time,

---

1. Luke 14,28-33.

tells us that ordinary Galileans 'hated Tiberias'.[1] Neither this city, nor the adjoining pleasure town, Magdala, were acceptable to the ordinary people.

Jesus, therefore, turned to the north of the lake. There lay a typically Jewish town, **Capernaum**.

Capernaum enjoyed a privileged position. One road ran along the shore from east to west, linking Phoenicia and Galilee with the regions across the Jordan. Another major road, the imperial highway, ran from the south, skirted around Capernaum and bent to Damascus in the north. In 1975 a milestone was found close to Capernaum with this inscription: '(Erected by) the Emperor, Traianus Adrianus Augustus, son of the divine Traianus Parthicus, nephew of the divine Nerva'. Coins found in Capernaum confirm its commercial links with many countries: Golan, Syria, Phoenicia, Asia Minor and Cyprus.

The Gospel mentions that Capernaum possessed a customs house, the one in which Levi, son of Alphaeus, worked as a commercial inspector.[2] The duties were collected here because Capernaum was a border town through which people entered the tetrarchy of Herod Antipas. The presence of a detachment of Roman soldiers in the town also underscores its strategic importance.[3]

---

1. FLAVIUS JOSEPHUS, *Life*, no 381 - 389; on Tiberias, see S.FREYNE, *Galilee from Alexander the Great to Hadrian*, Wilmington 1980, pp. 129 - 134.

2. Mark 2,13-14.

3. Matthew 8,5-13; Luke 7,1-10.

Capernaum would be an excellent choice. It would give Jesus a presence in the heartland of Galilean public life. It would provide easy access to the surrounding regions . . . .

Matthew tells us:

'Jesus left Nazareth
and settled in Capernaum,
in the land of Zebulun and Naphtali.'
Matthew 4,13

Capernaum became Jesus' residence.

'Jesus got into the boat
and went across the lake to his own town.'
Matthew 9,1

'Jesus went to Capernaum
and the news spread that he was at home.'
Mark 2,1

What about Capernaum itself? What kind of place was it? Can we visualise what it looked like? And how did Jesus go about building up new relationships?

Spying out the land

During the last century scholars debated the exact location of Capernaum.[1] Excavations and a renewed study of ancient literary sources allow us now to pinpoint the place exactly.

The town itself was not very big. Not more than 1000 people lived in it. But a large strip of land outside the town proper be-

---

1. See, for example, W.SANDAY who reviews the arguments at the time in *Sacred Sites of the Gospels*, Oxford 1903, pp.36 - 48.

longed to it: from the Jordan on the east to the spring of Ayn Tabgha on the west. Both the town and the land belonging to it, were often referred to by the same name.[1]

Flavius Josephus, who was governor of Galilee some forty years after Jesus' death, talks about the town in these terms:

'During the battle (at the mouth of the Jordan, north of lake Galilee) the horse I rode sank in boggy ground and threw me off. I was taken to *the village Capharnomon* with a bruised wrist.'[2]

He also mentions its land, and the spring Ayn Tabgha that waters the plain of Gennesaret.

'Apart from the lovely, warm climate, it is watered from a most fertilising spring. The local people call it *Capharnaum*. Some maintain the water of the spring could come from the Nile because it produces as much Coracin fish as the lake near Alexandria.'[3]

The spring (present-day Ayn Tabgha) was an outpost of Capernaum, a small 'industrial suburb'. That is why it, too, carried the name of Capernaum. Excavations have shown that there were mills; and other industries, such as potteries and tanneries. Water from the spring irrigated not only Capernaum's coastal strip, but, via a cemented channel cut through

1. W.SANDAY, 'The site of Capernaum', *Journal of Theological Studies* 5 (1904) pp. 42 - 48.

2. 'Capharnomon' is a Greek variant of the name; FLAVIUS JOSEPHUS, *Life*, c.72, no 403.

3. FLAVIUS JOSEPHUS, *Jewish Wars*, III, 10, 8; no 519, 520.

the rock, it also irrigated the nearby plain of Gennesaret.[1]

Jesus, however, settled in the main village, in the town of Capernaum itself. Recent excavations (1968 - 1984) have uncovered about half of the ancient site. My attempt at a reconstruction of the town will closely follow the latest archeological reports.[2]

The town

Capernaum covered only a few acres. We do not know its precise size at the time of Christ. Probably it was not more than 200 yards deep (from north to south, i.e. from the lake to the hills) and 300 yards wide along the shore of the lake (see the plan of part of the excavations on the opposite page).

Although remains of very early human occupation have been found underneath some houses, the town of Jesus' time had been founded in the 5th century BC. This means that it may well have begun as a small Persian settlement, established to control the trade routes along the northern shore of the lake. In the course of time Jews settled in the town, as petty officials, traders, skilled labourers and so on, forming, in the end, the

---

1. C.KOPP, *Die heiligen Stätten der Evangelien*, Regensburg 1959, pp. 215 - 220; *The Holy Places of the Gospels*, London 1964, pp. 171 - 177.

2. B.BAGATTI, 'Caphernaum, la ville de Pierre', *La Monde de la Bible* 27 (1983) pp. 8 - 16; V.TZAFERIS, 'New Archaeological Evidence on Ancient Capernaum' *Biblical Archaeologist* 48 (1985) pp. 207 - 216; S.LOFFREDA,*Caphamaum. The Town of Jesus*, Jerusalem 1984; *Recovering Caphamaum*, Jerusalem 1985.

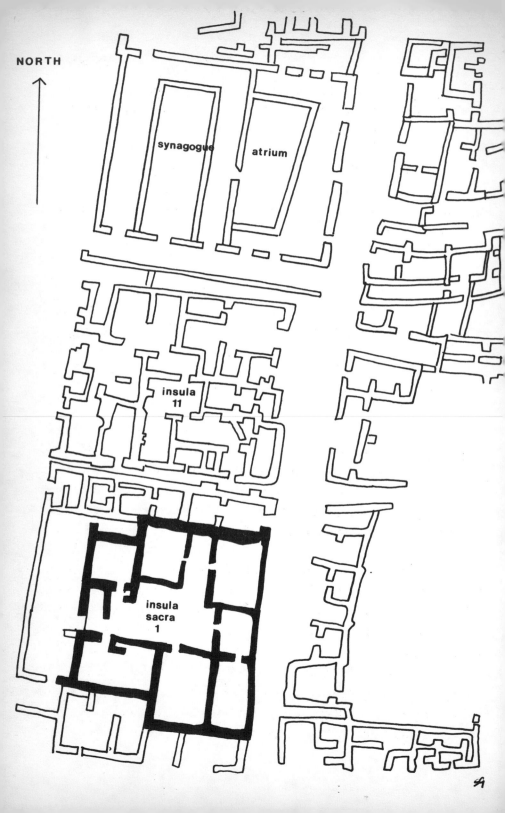

NORTH

synagogue

atrium

insula
11

insula
sacra
1

majority of its population. Under successive Greek and Roman colonial rulers Capernaum may have retained its character of a local government post.

This official character can still be seen in its systematic town plan (see opposite page). As in other Persian/Greek/Roman cities, there are main streets (here running from north to south) intersected by small alleys (that run from east to west). The result is a number of square blocks of houses.

The excavations revealed two places of special interest: a synagogue and a Christian shrine to mark St.Peter's house. Since both these places are of great concern to us, we will pay special attention to them later. The question we should consider first is: can we say anything more definite about the kind of people who lived in Capernaum in Jesus' time?

We can. One striking observation is that we do not find the great social contrasts that existed in other parts of Galilee. Almost all the houses have a similar design. We do not come across huge mansions next to tiny hovels. The citizens of Capernaum were middle-class people. Their houses were simple, but not poor by the standards of the time.

This confirms Capernaum's role as a government post and a trading centre. There were local industries too. Finished and unfinished olive presses have come to light, grinding stones for use in the homes, mortars, bowls and craters. This equipment, made of basalt stone, was manufactured in Capernaum itself. A workshop to produce glass vessels has also been unearthed. The fishing industry, too, was not as primitive as we sometimes imagine. Fish was transported to Tarichaeae (near Magdala) where it was dried and salted for export.

Of course, the town must have had its share of outcasts and underdogs; like the leper whom Jesus cured just outside the town[1] and the Roman officer's slave.[2] But on the whole the citizens of Capernaum were free citizens and skilled workers, ordinary people who had to work hard to make ends meet.

These were the people Jesus chose to become his close associates. How did he make his first friends among them? It is a story the Gospels and modern archaeology allow us to reconstruct with some precision.

The town becomes a home

It is likely that Jesus hired a room somewhere in or near Capernaum. On account of its position along a number of major roads, Capernaum must have had some inn or guest house for travellers to stay. The Gospel of John has preserved some traditions about these earliest days. John the Baptist was baptising near Bethany, on the east side of the river Jordan.[3] That may well have been on the banks of the Jordan north of the lake of Galilee. That would explain why fishermen from Capernaum and Bethsaida were the Baptist's disciples at the time.

John the Baptist told his followers he had seen the Spirit come down on Jesus.[4] Impressed by this testimony, two of

---

1. Matthew 8,1-4; Mark 1,40-45.

2. Matthew 8,5-13; Luke 7,1-10.

3. John 1,28.

4. John 1,29-34.

John's audience walked up behind Jesus, desirous to meet him.

Jesus turned round and saw they were following him.

'What are you looking for?' he asked.

They answered: 'Where do you live, Teacher?'

'Come and see', Jesus replied.

It was about four o'clock in the afternoon. They walked along with him, saw where he lived and spent the rest of the day with him.'

John 1,37-39

The Gospel then tells us that one of these two first disciples was Andrew. Andrew took his brother, Simon, to meet Jesus. Jesus gave him the new name *Cephas* (in Aramaic) or *Peter* (in Greek), i.e. 'Rock'.[1] Peter and Andrew were fishermen. Jesus invited them to leave their fishing nets and join him as 'fishermen of people'.[2] It must have been a time of an intense common search. Jesus explained his vision and obtained the first personal commitments.

All the evidence we have now points to a new development: Peter invited Jesus to stay in his house. Leaving his temporary place in the travellers' lodge, Jesus moved into a room in Peter's house. As we know from the excavations in Capernaum and elsewhere, an ordinary 'house' consisted of a number of rooms clustered round a courtyard. Each room would accommodate a family. Relatives would tend to join together. This gave more security: there was a common entrance to the courtyard and cooking facilities in the yard were shared.

---

1. John 1,40-42.

2. Mark 1,16-18; Matthew 4,18-20; Luke 5,1-11.

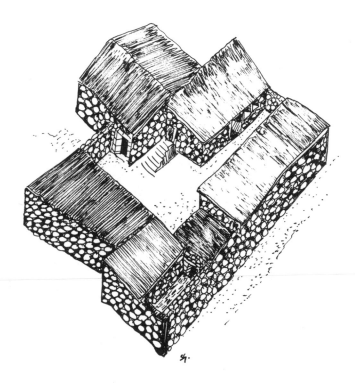

Plan of the courtyard underlying 'Peter's shrine'.
No 1. The special room that became the centre of the shrine. Was this where Jesus stayed?
No 2 - 6. Other living rooms. Here the families of Peter and Andrew may have lived.

Pilgrims to Palestine in the early centuries are known to have visited a place in Capernaum which they believed was 'Peter's house', 'the house where Jesus lived'. Archaeology has now found that house. As is common with ancient shrines, in the course of the centuries ever more elaborate monuments were built on top of one another (see the historical survey on page 43). The great interest for us is that it gives us quite an accurate picture of what the house was like in Jesus' time.[1]

One entered St.Peter's house, if we may call it such for a moment, through a gate from the main north-south street (see plan on opposite page). Inside was an L-shaped courtyard. It gave access to six rooms, of which the one immediately left of the gate was the special room, the room later venerated as a shrine. This was, perhaps, Jesus' own room. The courtyard had grinding stones and a fireplace, and a flight of stone stairs leading up to its roof. All the rooms could only be entered from the courtyard.

On the whole the rooms were rather narrow and dark. The walls were built up from rough basalt stones placed upon each other, poorly cemented together with a mixture of mud and pebbles. The walls were weak and could not be drawn up higher than nine feet. The rooms received light from small windows that looked out onto the courtyard. The roofs consisted of wooden beams covered by a plaster of beaten earth mixed with straw. In some cases, when the roof was used for space to

---

1. Even if it were not to be the actual place where Jesus lived (though its credentials are excellent!), it helps us visualise what Jesus' residence was like. All houses in Capharnaum are similar in type.

History of Peter's house as a shrine based on archaeological excavations

1.   The central, oldest room dates from *the first century AD*. It was part of the usual type of 'courtyard house'. From the end of the first century it was used for prayers and religious meetings. Rabbinical sources confirm that there was a Christian Jewish community at Capernaum at the time. The room must have been **a sacred shrine** for them.

2.   *In the fourth century* Greek pilgrims built a **sanctuary** on the same spot. A large enclosure wall was constructed around the central, oldest room. The room was redecorated with frescoes of geometrical figures, flowers, branches, trees and so on. More than 150 inscriptions were found on the walls, calling on Jesus as the Lord. The pilgrim Etheria (385 AD) described the sanctuary in these words: 'In Capernaum the house of the prince of the apostles (St.Peter) has been made into a church. Its walls still stand today as they were'.

3.   Byzantine Christians built **an octagonal Church** over it *in the fifth century*. A pilgrim from Piacenza visited it in 570 AD :'We arrived at Capernaum in Blessed Peter's house. At present it is a basilica'. It was probably destroyed by the Persians in 614 AD and remained a ruin ever since.

Since the tradition is so old, it is very likely that this room was remembered as the place (in Peter's house) where Jesus stayed.

sit on or to support a second floor, the beams were stronger and covered with flat tiles.

It is here that various incidents related in the Gospels come to life.

Leaving the synagogue, Jesus went, with James and John, straight to the house of Peter and Andrew. Simon's mother-in-law was sick in bed with a fever. They informed Jesus about this immediately. He went to her, took her by the hand and helped her up. The fever left her and she began to wait on them.

That evening, after sunset, people brought to Jesus all the sick and those possessed by demons. The whole town crowded round the door. He healed many who were suffering from all kinds of diseases.

Mark 1,29-34

After one of his missionary tours, Jesus came back to Capernaum. 'The news spread that he was at home.' Many people came to see him. He talked to them in his house. Four men arrived, who must have been from a neighbouring village. They were carrying a paralysed relative on a mat. Because of the crowd they could not get near to Jesus. So they climbed up the stairs leading to the roof. 'Then they made a hole in the roof right above the place where Jesus was. Through the opening they let the man down, lying on his mat.' Jesus was impressed by their faith. He talked to the paralysed man, forgave him his sins and cured him.

Read *Mark 2,1-12*!

Again, another time, when Jesus returned with his apostles, he taught them privately a lesson in the seclusion of his own home. 'They came to Capernaum'. After going indoors he asked his disciples: 'What were you arguing about on the road?' They

St. Peter's Courtyard

South

North

*Reconstruction of Peter's courtyard. The room at
the left hand top may have been the room where
Jesus stayed. It became the centre of the later
shrine.*

   *Practically all the houses in Capernaum must
have looked like this.*

did not give any reply, but he knew they had been quarrelling about who among them held the highest rank. So Jesus sat down, made a child stand in their middle and told them: 'Whoever wants to be first, must become like a child.' He embraced the child and blessed it.

Read *Mark 9,33-37.*

The collectors of the Temple tax came to Capernaum, we are told. They asked Peter: 'Will your master not pay the tax?' 'Of course, he will', Peter replied. He entered the house, probably intending to pay for Jesus. But Jesus knew what had happened. He told Peter that strictly speaking he was exempt from the tax; but that, in order to avoid difficulties, it would be better to pay the tax from the day's catch of fish.[1]

Read *Matthew 17,24-27.*

Having moved in with Peter, Jesus soon became a local resident of Capernaum. By intense, everyday sharing of life he could create the deep, personal relationships that formed the beginning of the Church. From his new home his message spread to ever wider circles.

Preaching in the synagogue

From what the Gospels tell us, we know that Capernaum possessed a synagogue and that Jesus regularly took part in its services.

Jesus and the apostles came to Capernaum. As soon

---

1. The sign of the tax coin found in the fish's mouth will be explained in the WALKING ON WATER book *the Resurrection.*

45

as it was Sabbath, Jesus went to the synagogue and
began to teach.

Mark 1,21.

He taught this doctrine at Capernaum, in the synagogue there.

John 6,71

Synagogues are prayer halls where Jews meet on the Sabbath day to pray and to listen to readings from the Bible.[1] In
Jesus' days synagogues already portrayed all the essential features we know today. They were simple, rectangular structures,
with benches around the sides, and a pulpit. In an alcove that
could be curtained off, an 'ark' was kept that held the Bible
scrolls.

Among the ruins of Capernaum, under a building of a later
date, the synagogue of Jesus' time has been rediscovered (see
the survey of its history on the opposite page). We can be quite
sure that this was the place Jesus knew. The Gospels always
speak of *the* synagogue and no similar structure was found
elsewhere among the ruins.[2]

Basing ourselves on the archaeological evidence, we can
visualise what the synagogue looked like. It was a longish hall,
18 meters (54 feet) long and 8 meters (24 feet) wide. It could
accommodate from 70 to 100 people. The Torah may have been
read from the southern wall, so that the congregation faced in
the direction of Jerusalem. Probably the synagogue had one
main entrance and small windows along the walls. Both the

----

1. More information about this in the WALKING ON WATER
course *Religion of the Heart*.

2. J.STRANGE and H.SHARKS, 'Synagogue where Jesus
preached found at Capernaum', *The Bulletin of Archaeological
Research* 9 (1983) pp. 24 - 31.

History of Capernaum's Synagogue based on archaeological excavations

1. The oldest part are houses from the early Hellenistic era (third and second century BC).

2. *In the first century AD* a simple rectangular synagogue was constructed. Of this, the floor, made of basalt stones, and the lower part of some walls still remain.

3. *In the fourth century* a larger, and more beautiful, synagogue was constructed over the earlier one. Heavy, well-carved, limestone blocks were used for the walls and the facade. Its columns and lintels were decorated with elaborate stone carvings. Many coins were found in a treasury belonging to this time. The pilgrim Etheria (385 AD) was impressed. 'One enters the synagogue by many steps. It has been built from square stones'. Some Jewish historians think the Emperor Julian the Apostate (361-363 AD) paid for its construction. He tried to suppress Christianity among other ways by encouraging Judaism.[1]

4. *In the fifth century* additional rooms were added to the building.

5. Like St.Peter's shrine, the whole edifice was probably destroyed by the Persians in their campaign of 614 AD.

1. W.ZANGER, ' A visit to the Kinneret', *Bible Times* 1 (1988) pp. 74-81.

door and the shutters for the windows were made of wood.

When Jesus took part in the services, he may have been invited to do a reading and provide commentary. This would give him an opportunity to preach the Good News. Also after the services, if the synagogue was left open, Jesus could continue to speak to whoever wanted to listen to him.

Jesus taught with authority and not like the scribes, the Gospels tell us. That is why he made a deep impression on people in Capernaum.[1] He also performed miracles in this synagogue, such as the healing of a man possessed by an unclean spirit.[2] Through such activity Jesus must have steadily widened the circle of his followers. Reports of what Jesus did 'spread throughout the region'.[3]

The Roman officer who was stationed in Capernaum wanted Jesus to cure his slave. The man was seriously ill. Instead of approaching Jesus directly, he sent some of the Jewish elders to plead on his behalf. The elders mention an interesting fact. 'This Roman deserves a favour', they said to Jesus. 'He is friendly towards our people. He is the one who built the synagogue'.[4]

What exactly did the officer do? Did he put up money for the building? Did he help by granting the necessary permissions? Or did he order his soldiers to execute the construction work? After all, soldiers were taught to build fortifications, and spanning the prayer hall with wide enough wooden girders must

---

1. Mark 1,22; Luke 4,31-32.

2. Mark 1,23-28; Luke 4,33-36.

3. Luke 4,37.

4. Luke 7,1-10.

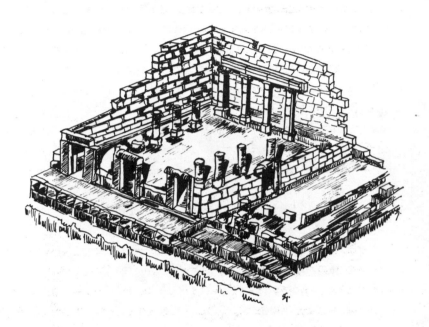

First Century Synagogue

*From the excavations in Capernaum and else-
where, we know that synagogues in Jesus' time
had a simple plan. After entering one of the doors,
one saw a central nave surrounded by colonnades.
The three side aisles contained benches for seating the worshippers.*

have required special skills. It is an interesting example of Roman-Jewish cooperation. It also shows that the synagogue was a recent acquisition for the town.

It was in this synagogue in Capernaum that Jesus argued with the people about his own role.[1] Many were not prepared to believe that he was the new 'bread that comes down from heaven'. 'This teaching is too hard . . . . Who can listen to it?' A large number of people turned away from Jesus.[2] The lines of division were beginning to be drawn.

Friendly and hostile responses

Jesus' demand for conversion and for the acceptance of new standards in the kingdom of his Father, pleased some people and displeased others. The case of the repentant tax collector illustrates the point.

Levi, son of Alphaeus, was an inspector of custom duties, attached to the tax house along the road near Capernaum. At Jesus' words 'Follow me!', he left his job and became one of Jesus' disciples. Many of the orthodox Jews were scandalised. When Levi organised a meal for Jesus in his home, they complained: 'See, he eats with criminals and tax collectors!'[3]

---

1. John 6,25-59.

2. John 6,60.66.

3. Mark 2,13-17; Luke 5,27-32; in Matthew 9,9-13 he is called Matthew.

Jairus, one of the men in charge of the synagogue, asked Jesus to come to his home and heal his little daughter. When they arrived at the house, they found mourning had begun because the girl had died. Jesus said she was asleep. They laughed and mocked him. Jesus had to turn them out of the room before he could cure the girl.[1]

Capernaum was the town where Jesus recruited his first band of supporters. It was also the centre of the first core of opposition. The bustling, hard-working, flourishing town at the north end of the lake had its fair share of pride and inflexibility.

After complaining about the neighbouring towns, Chorazin and Bethsaida, Jesus also warned Capernaum.

> **'And what about you, Capernaum?**
> **Will you be exalted to heaven?**
> **You will be thrown down to hell!**
> **If the miracles performed in you had been done in**
> **Sodom, it would still stand today!**
> **I tell you, on judgment day God will have more**
> **mercy with Sodom than with you!'**
> *Matthew 11,23-24*

They were the prophetic words of a man concerned about people he had come to consider his own.

---

1. Mark 5,21-23.35-43; Matthew 9,18-19.23-26.

QUESTIONS FOR PERSONAL STUDY

1. Jesus chose Capernaum as the centre for his public ministry.
> **'Jesus left Nazareth and took residence in Caper-**
> **naum, in the land of Zebulun and Naphtali . . . .'**
> *Matthew 4,13.*

Why did Jesus not 'think big'? Like establishing himself in Tiberias (the capital of Galilee), Jerusalem (the capital for all Jews) or Rome (the capital of the Roman Empire)?

2. Jesus often received people in his home.
> **'Where do you live teacher?' they said.**
> **'Come and see', Jesus replied . . . .**
> **They saw where he lived and spent the rest of the day**
> **with him.**
> *John 1,38-39*

What can we learn from Jesus' pastoral practice?

3. Right from the beginning Jesus encouraged others to join him in his mission. Comment on Jesus' strategy in the light of this text from Vatican II:
> **When people work, they do not only change things**
> **and society, they develop themselves as well. They**
> **learn much, cultivate their resources, go outside**
> **themselves and beyond themselves.**
> **Rightly understood this kind of growth is of greater**
> **value than any external achievement. People are more**
> **precious for what they *are* than for what they *have*.**
> *The Church in the Modern World*, no 35.

Space for your own notes

Chapter Two

NAZARETH

Jesus' stay in the business town of Capernaum did not make him forget the people in the country side. We are told that he went round 'visiting all the towns and villages'.[1] He visited all the villages around Capernaum.[2] People would put their sick on the ground in open places, begging him to allow them to touch the hem of his garment, 'in whatever villages, towns or small hamlets Jesus entered'.[3] And when Jesus sent his disciples out in twos to preach the Kingdom, he expected them to call on even the tiniest village.[4]

Jesus knew what villages were like. He himself had lived in Nazareth.

What kind of place was Nazareth?

It was such a small hamlet that it is not mentioned in any historical sources outside the Gospels. Not once is it referred to in the Old Testament books. Flavius Josephus, who describes the war between the Jews and Romans in Galilee (67-68 AD),

---

1. Matthew 9,35; cf. Luke 8,1.

2. Mark 6,6.

3. Mark 6,56.

4. Matthew 10,11; cf. Luke 10,1.

mentions 200 Galilean towns and villages by name. Nazareth is not among them. Also the Talmud and other contemporary Jewish sources do not mention it; its name only occurs in some second-century texts.

From this we can already deduce that Nazareth was indeed small; so small and insignificant, in fact, that even most Galileans had never heard of it. It explains Nathanael's reaction when Peter told him: 'We have met the person announced by Moses and the prophets. It is Jesus, son of Joseph, from Nazareth'.

'From Nazareth?!' Nathanael exclaimed. 'Can anything good come from Nazareth?'[1]

It prepares us for the findings of archeological studies.

Nazareth in Jesus' day

The precise location of Nazareth has been preserved for us by Jewish settlements there after the wars with Rome. Nazareth lay in the lower hills just north of the plains of Esdraelon valley. It lay close to two large cities: Sephphoris, three miles to its north and Japha, one-and-a-half miles to its southwest. The major road from Egypt to Damascus ran six miles south of Nazareth through the valley of Esdraelon. Nazareth's position in a small valley of its own, tucked away behind stony hills (see the map of Galilee on page 19), kept it hidden and out of view.

Excavations show that Nazareth was not a recent foundation. Tombs have been found with pottery and ornaments that can be dated back to the Middle Bronze Age (2000 - 1550 BC), the Late Bronze Age (1550 - 1200 BC) and the Iron Age (1200 -

---

1. John 1,45-46.

View of Nazareth

587 BC). Different populations must have lived here, spanning the transition from the original Canaanites to the Israelites.

The tombs do not point to numerous inhabitants. The tombs have only been preserved better than elsewhere because Nazareth lay on limestone from which they were hewn. Nazareth had to remain small for two reasons: the surrounding area was stony and arid, yielding no more than meagre crops; and it possessed only one tiny well, with a scant supply of water.

Excavations show that in Jesus' days Nazareth lay on a small limestone outcrop that still forms the centre of Nazareth today.[1] It occupied an area of about a hundred yards long by fifty yards wide. Not more than twenty to thirty houses stood on this site (see the previous page for a reconstructed view). Underneath the houses and around them, caves had been hewn in the rock which served as silos to store grain, as cellars for wine and as cisterns to collect rain water.[2]

Nazareth's underground storage caves are a somewhat unusual feature. They were a bonus for the village, no doubt due to the favourable nature of the rock it stood on. The purposes for which the caves were used, show that the inhabi-

---

1. Some archaeologists thought that the tombs found in the central part, would exclude it from being the site of the ancient village. Jews would not live in a cemetery. The excavations of S.Bagatti (1960 - 1968) established that the tombs are much older. In all likelihood they were no longer known as tombs in Jesus' day. At that time the cemetery lay more to the south.

2. The discovery of the underground caves in the Middle Ages led to the belief that the people of Nazareth lived in them (Burchard of Mount Sion in 1283 AD). This was not the case. The people lived in simple stone houses which stood over the cellars and in between the water cisterns. S.LOFFREDA, 'Nazareth à l'époque évangélique', *Le Monde de la Bible*, no 56, Paris 1980.

tants of Nazareth lived from agriculture: from vineyards, olive groves, the cultivation of grains and some other basic crops. Jesus' Nazareth was a cluster of twenty farm houses, probably arranged in close formation to provide a maximum of protection against thieves and robbers. It was a mere speck on the map of Galilee, a place no one would have noticed if it had not been Jesus' home. 'Of Nazareth' was Jesus' *family* name.[1]

Jesus' relatives

The people of Nazareth must, in fact, have constituted a clan of interrelated families. Mary, Jesus' mother, lived in Nazareth before her marriage to Joseph.[2] Joseph must have lived in Nazareth too, for he 'took her to his home' to complete their marriage.[3] During one of Jesus' visits to Nazareth the people say about him:

'Where did he get this wisdom and miraculous powers?
Isn't he the builder's son?
Is Mary not his mother and aren't James, Joseph, Simon and Jude his brothers?
Do all his sisters not live among us?
Where did he get all this from?'
Matthew 13,54-56

---

1. The inscription on Jesus' cross, in three languages: Hebrew, Latin and Greek, identified the convict as 'Jesus of Nazareth'; John 19,19-20.

2. Luke 1,26.

3. Matthew 1,18.20.24.

If, as we may presume, his brothers and sisters (= Jesus' cousins in Semitic speech) were by then married and lived in their own homes, Jesus was related to half the population of Nazareth!

Disaster was to strike the village hardly forty years later, when the Roman armies ravaged the countryside in their campaign against nearby Japha (67 AD). Flavius Josephus recounts that the Romans placed 7000 troops in Sephphoris who systematically plundered the surrounding valleys, killing all the able-bodied men and selling the others as slaves. Villagers found refuge in the fortress of Japha for some time; when this city fell, all survivors met a similar fate.[1]

What happened to Jesus' relatives?

Some must have died with their fellow Galileans. Others escaped because, as the early historian Eusebius claims,[2] they had scattered from Nazareth all over the land. We know for a fact that some were part of the early Christian congregation in Jerusalem. One of their first bishops, James, was called 'a brother (relative) of the Lord'[3] and Cleophas[4] was also related to Christ, as tradition tells us. Some of Jesus' relatives worked as Christian missionaries.[5] It is likely that the names of Jesus' brothers quoted above - James, Joseph, Simon and Jude - were so easily recalled in tradition because the early Christians knew them.

---

1. *Jewish Wars* III 4,1; 7,32.

2. EUSEBIUS (265 - 340 AD),*History of the Church* I 7,14; edition by LAWLOR and OULTON, London 1927.

3. Galatians 1,19.

4. Luke 24,18.

5. 1 Corinthians 9,5.

Did some of Jesus' family return to Nazareth after the wars with Rome?

The evidence seems against it.

We know that a priestly clan from Jerusalem settled there who made it a stronghold of Jewish, anti-Christian resistance.[1] We do find the story of St.Konon, who died as a martyr in Pamphylia in 249 AD. He is said to have stated before a Roman judge: 'I am from Nazareth in Galilee. I am a relative of Christ whom I and my ancestors have served'.[2] But his origin from Nazareth does not prove that he actually lived there; any more than Joseph's being 'from Bethlehem'[3] proves that he lived in Bethlehem. Epiphanius heard from Joseph of Tiberias (359 AD) that no Greek, Samaritan or Christian lived in Nazareth, 'because the Jewish inhabitants do not tolerate any stranger among them'.[4]

A builder's view of Nazareth

We have no continuous Christian tradition in Nazareth. Moreover, no sure archaeological evidence was found of Christian veneration there until the fourth century. This means we cannot be sure that the present shrines in Nazareth mark the

---

1. S.K.KLEIN, *Beiträge zur Geographie und Geschichte Galiläas*, Leipzig 1909, p.94.

2. A.P.KERAMEUS, *Analekta*, Petersburg 1898, vol. 5, p.386.

3. Luke 2,2-3.

4. *Against the Heretics*, XXX 11,9-10; C.KOPP, *Die heiligen Stætten der Evangelien*, Regensburg 1959, p. 90.

The village 'carpenter', the handyman, did a thousand and one odd jobs, requiring a variety of skills. He was an indispensable member of any village community.

exact location of Mary's or Joseph's home;[1] or, for that matter, of the synagogue in Jesus' time.

However, this does not constitute much of a loss. The area of ancient Nazareth is so small and so well defined, that the exact location of one home or the other makes little difference. They were all so close together: Mary's ancestral home, the house of Joseph and Mary where Jesus grew up, the small building that served as synagogue and the houses of relatives and friends. All were within shouting distance.

The layout of a village like Nazareth, we can be sure, had not been planned. There was no real centre; only two focal points: the house of prayer and the well, four hundred yards south of the village. There were no proper streets; only passages between houses or their compound walls.

It is commonly believed that Jesus was a carpenter. The word used in the Gospels, however, actually means *builder*; it designates any craftsman who works in wood, stone or metal. In a place like Nazareth it included everything in the nature of building or maintenance. Jesus was called the 'son of Joseph, the builder'[2] or simply 'the builder'.[3] In our terms he was building contractor, stone mason, carpenter and smith all rolled into one. He was the village handyman.

Jesus knew all the houses in Nazareth, because he had either built them or repaired them. A peasant's house usually consisted of just one rectangular room, of about 12 to 16 square yards (12 feet x 14 feet). In Nazareth the walls were built with small limestone blocks. The roofs were constructed by laying brush-

---

1. For contrary claims, read F.MANNS and J.DAOUST in *Le Monde de la Bible*, no 16, Paris 1980, pp.16 - 28.

2. Matthew 13,55.

3. Mark 6,3.

wood across sycamore beams, covering the surface with compressed and dried mud. The house had an entrance that could be closed by a wooden door, and one or two small, square windows.

The floor space inside the room was divided into two parts. The area close to the door was made of stamped-down earth. Here stood the household utensils and the farmer's tools. Here was the fireplace, if cooking or heating needed to be done indoors. The other half of the floor consisted of a slightly raised, stone platform for family activities, such as eating and sleeping.

A low boundary wall in front of the house or beside it was used to enclose domestic animals during the night. Here, too, were the cisterns for rainwater and the silos discovered in the excavations. Stone steps led from inside the enclosure to the roof. From here steps also led down into the cellars, if a house possessed one.

Jesus' experience as a builder shows up in some of the comparisons he uses.

* A man may well build a house on sand during the dry season and believe all is well. But when the rain and the wind lash against the house, the walls will collapse. Only a house built on rock will stand.[1]

* Jesus gave Simon the Aramaic name *Cephas*, that is: rock ('Peter' in Greek); he wanted to build his Church on Peter's strength.[2]

* A man who wants to build a two-story house must realise that the foundations and the walls need to be specially reinforced. He should calculate this extra cost beforehand, otherwise he will not be able to complete

1. Matthew 7,24-27; Luke 6,47-49

2. John 1,42; Matthew 16,18.

Since building materials lacked today's strength (there was no steel or cement), the solidity of a house depended on how stones and wood were fitted together. It required careful planning and real craftsmanship.

the building and his neighbours will laugh at him.[1]

* An unwieldy stone rejected by the builders as unsuitable for the walls, may well turn out to be excellent as a corner stone.[2] Then it can give support to two or three walls at once.

Everyday life

The people of Nazareth worked on the land. They either possessed an orchard or vineyard themselves, or held such properties as tenants for rich landowners, as I will explain later (in chapter seven). Jesus too must have spent many days working on the land when all hands were required, to prune vines or gather in the harvest. But at other times he went round doing a hundred different jobs: repairing a roof, hewing out a cistern, carving a new plough. The people may have paid him in kind; with a measure of grain, oil or figs.

The women in the village would share in the farming as much as they could. Part of their day was spent in fetching water from the well, grinding corn and preparing food for the family. The menfolk would return at nightfall. They would secure their goats and sheep, and join the women for the evening meal. The daily routine was quite demanding since even simple jobs required a lot of hard, physical work. There was little time for leisure. Contacts with outsiders were limited to visits from family and friends living in other towns, and to the annual pilgrimage to Jerusalem.

In almost every respect Jesus must have lived like the other people in his village. But there was a difference. From an early

---

1. Luke 14,28-30.

2. Mark 12,10.

age he must have done a lot of thinking and praying. Nazareth lay in a secluded place, and yet it looked out upon a wider world. During the few occasions I have been privileged to visit Nazareth, I spent time roaming the countryside around it. What struck me is the magnificent views it offers. From a summit above the village one looks south across the beautiful plain of Jezreel, west to Mount Carmel on the Mediterranean coast and east to Mount Tabor. On a clear day one can even see, in the far north, the snow- capped tip of Mount Hermon. Jesus must have sat there and thought about the world he belonged to.

Luke has preserved a tradition according to which the twelve-years old boy Jesus asked amazing questions of the scribes in the Temple of Jerusalem.[1] They must have been related to Scripture. Jesus had learned to read and write. Every Jewish community that possessed a synagogue would make sure a number of intelligent lads were taught the Hebrew alphabet so that they could become readers on the sabbath day. Jesus was one of them.

Jesus studied nature, 'the work of his Father',[2] and the Father's word, the inspired Scriptures.[3] But he also studied people. For people would be his main concern.

---

1. Luke 2,41-52.

2. Matthew 6,25-32; John 5,17.

3. Compare John 5,39-40.

Jesus' reception in Nazareth

The people of Nazareth had heard news of what Jesus was doing in Capernaum. His obvious success as a preacher and healer intrigued them. It was something they had never expected from their quiet, unassuming 'handyman'! What was he up to? Where did he get his unusual powers from?

During one of his visits to his home village, Jesus joined them on the sabbath for prayer in the synagogue. When he was asked to read, he took the opportunity to explain his mission. He chose[1] Isaiah 61,1-2 for this purpose.

'The Spirit of the Lord is upon me.'

> *'What I am doing, I do through the Father's power. He has called me as he called so many prophets in the past.'*

'He has chosen me to bring good news to the poor.

> *'The Father sent me to ordinary people with a message that will make them happy.'*

'He commissions me to proclaim freedom for captives
> **and sight for the blind,**
to set the oppressed free
and announce the Lord's year of grace.'

> *'Through me the Father begins the messianic liberation promised by his prophets.'*

Jesus states clearly that he is the Messiah the Jews were waiting for - something his relatives may have found hard to swallow. And he says that his mission is to help *people*. The liberation and salvation of *people* is his priority. This, too, irked

---

1. Luke 4,17. The *imperfect* form of the Greek verb shows it means: 'he looked for', not 'he found'.

his former companions since he seemed to favour 'outsiders'.

The prophecies of Isaiah Jesus quoted from, speak a lot about restoring Israel's fortunes as a nation and of rebuilding Jerusalem in all its glory.[1] Jesus deliberately chose the section that speaks of freeing and saving the people that are in need: the poor, the blind, the oppressed, the tenants who are in prison because they cannot pay off their debt. Jesus did not come to create new institutions. He came for people.

'Why don't you perform miracles among us, as you did in Capernaum?' they wanted to know.

'I would, if only you would believe in me', he replied.[2]

'Why do you do more for strangers, for 'outsiders' than for us?' they insisted.

'The outsiders have faith. Faith is more important to the Father than blood relationship. That is why Elijah provided food for the widow who lived in Sidon, and not for widows in Israel. Elisha cured Naaman, a leper from Syria, but no Jewish lepers.[3] Moreover, prophets are never recognised in their home land.'[4]

The people became angry. They dragged him out of the synagogue and 'took him to the top of the hill on which their village was built. They wanted to throw him down the cliff'.[5] The meaning of this is clear. They considered his messianic claim a blasphemy. They decided to punish him with the prescribed penalty, namely stoning the blasphemer to death. Such stoning

---

1. See Isaiah 60,1-22; 61,10 - 62,12.

2. Mark 6,5-6.

3. Luke 4,25-27.

4. Luke 4,24.

5. Luke 4,29.

was begun by throwing the culprit down from some height, then crushing him with stones. The natural place for such an execution was a steep cliff on one side of the village. Jesus, however, walked away through the middle of the crowd and left.

The violent reaction of Jesus' village folk gives us an idea of the fanaticism with which the ordinary people clung to their religious convictions.[1] For the early Christians the event foreshadowed the even more tragic rejection of Jesus by Israel as a whole. Jesus' words about a prophet not being welcome in his own land, would take on much wider implications. For Jesus, however, it was a question of principle that he had come not to gratify his own relatives, but to serve people in need. They should have known.

Even before the clash in Nazareth itself, he had made this plain. While he was teaching a crowd of people in his house in Capernaum,[2] a group of his relatives, accompanied by his mother, tried to get priority attention. Probably they expected Jesus to dismiss the others and entertain them instead.

'See, your mother and your brothers and sisters are standing outside. They're asking for you!'

'Who is my mother? Who are my relatives?' Jesus replied. Then pointing at the people sitting around him he said: 'Look! Here are my mother and my relatives. Whoever does the will of God is my brother, my sister, my mother.'

Mark 3,32-35

---

1. There may have been political motives as well as I will explain later.

2. Mark 3,31; see 3,20.

One of the radical demands of Jesus' mission was that he value people in their own right; not because they were related to him or shared a common interest. The first priority in God's Kingdom was, and is, people.

QUESTIONS FOR PERSONAL STUDY

1. The Gospel records this incident:
> **A woman said to him: 'Blessed the womb that bore you and the breasts that you sucked.'**
> **Jesus replied: 'Rather, blessed are those who listen to God's word and obey it!'**
> *Luke 11,27-28.*

What is Jesus saying here about his relationship to people?

2. In the light of Jesus' reception in Nazareth, and later in Jerusalem, what did these words mean to Jesus?
> **'The stone which the builders rejected has become the corner stone.**
> **This is God's doing; it's a wonderful thing in our eyes.'**
> *Psalm 118; see Matthew 21,42.*

3. In the light of what Jesus said about his mission in Nazareth (read Luke 4,16-21), comment on this passage from Vatican II:
> **'The joys and the hopes, the sorrows and the worries of the people of our time, especially of those who are poor or in any way afflicted, these too are the joys and hopes, the sorrows and worries of the followers of Christ. Indeed, nothing genuinely human can fail to raise an echo in their hearts.'**
> *The Church in the Modern World,* no 1.

Space for your own notes

Geog. — secluded — outward looking
privacy — (God) prayer

Ed. — thinking praying
reading synagogue — chose ..
Isaiah
— people — main concern.
~~family~~

Parables — → people — (men)
used later. in parables

He met opposition

3 — Given the limitations of Nazareth
(geography, education, culture, etc)
how was Jesus enabled to
"increase in wisdom,
in stature
- in favour with God & men"?

(Lk 2:52)

HEBREW AND ARAMAIC

If we had lived in Capernaum in Jesus' time, we might well have been surprised at the confusion of languages in that little town. Following Jesus into the synagogue on a sabbath morning, we would have heard the Old Testament scripture read out in Hebrew. Then we would have heard Jesus preach in Aramaic. When the Roman officer came to plead for his slave, we would have heard him make his plea in Greek.[1] Palestine in those days reverberated with the sound of many languages.

Some languages were ancient dialects spoken by neighbouring communities, such as Phoenician and Nabatean. Then there was Latin, the language of the Romans, used by the Roman authorities in Palestine for some of their administration.[2] But the three most important languages were Aramaic, Hebrew and Greek.

Greek had been introduced to Palestine during the two centuries of Greek occupation. Greek was *the* international language at the time. Greek was spoken by many citizens of the new, 'modern' cities that had been built in Palestine, such as Tiberias, Sephphoris, Scythopolis, Caesarea, and many others.

---

1. Matthew 8,5-13; Luke 7,1-10.

2. That is why Jesus' condemnation was written on the cross *also* in Latin (see John 19,20).

73

Greek was spoken by the Jewish communities outside Palestine and would become the main language of communication for the Early Church.[1] But did Jesus himself use Greek in his preaching ministry?

No one today can doubt the fact that many people in Palestine spoke Greek; even that there were groups of *Jews* for whom it was the only or principal language.[2] The 'Greeks' among the Christians in Jerusalem may have been such a group.[3] But it would be wrong to conclude from this that Greek was the language Jesus himself used, as some scholars have done.[4]

Like many of his contemporaries, Jesus must have known a smattering of Greek. He will have used it on some occasions; for instance, when he was approached by Greeks in Jerusalem, as John tells us.[5] Jesus may have spoken Greek in his exchange with Pilate; Greek was the language the Romans employed for such public transactions.[6] But these were exceptions. Jesus

---

1. Much more will be said about this in our WALKING ON WATER book *The Gospel transcends barriers*.

2. S.LIEBERMANN, *Greek in Jewish Palestine*, New York 1965; J.N.SEVENSTER, *Do you know Greek? How much Greek could the first Jewish Christians have known?*, Leiden 1968.

3. Acts 6,1 - 7; C.F.D.MOULE, 'Who were the Hellenists?', *Expository Times* 70 (1958-59) pp. 100 - 102.

4. See S.M.PATTERSON, 'What language did Jesus speak?', *Classical Outlook* 23 (1946) pp. 65-67; A.W.ARGYLE, 'Did Jesus speak Greek?', *Expository Times* 67 (1955-56) pp.92-93.

5. John 12,20.

6. John 18,33-38.

addressed himself to ordinary Jews.[1] And ordinary Jews, we can be sure, spoke either Aramaic or a colloquial form of Hebrew.[2] It is these two languages we will now discuss in more detail.

The origin of two sister languages

Hebrew and Aramaic belong to the family of languages called 'Semitic'. Hebrew and Aramaic are closely related to each other. They have many words in common. They share a good deal of grammar and syntax. In the time of Abraham (1850 BC?) they must have been almost identical. In an ancient prayer the patriarchs are called 'wandering Arameans'.[3] But the same mother tongue gave birth, in later centuries (1100 - 722 BC), to two distinct languages: Hebrew among the Jews in Palestine, and Aramaic in the Aramean kingdoms of Mesopotamia: Damascus, Zobah and Hamath.

Hebrew was the language spoken by Saul and David, by Isaiah, Jeremiah and the other prophets. Most of the Old Testament books were written in Hebrew. Though Hebrew changed in the course of the centuries - as languages invariably do, it retained its official place in Israel until the fall of Jerusalem in 587 BC. This is known as *classical Hebrew*.

---

1. Matthew 10,5-6; 15,24.

2. The findings of modern research, with plentiful detail and abundant bibliography, are provided by: J.A.FITZMEYER, 'The languages of Palestine in the First Century AD', *Catholic Biblical Quarterly* 32 (1970) pp.501-531; and C.RABIN, 'Hebrew and Aramaic in the First Century', in *The Jewish People in the First Century*, ed. S.SAFRAI and M.STERN, Leiden 1976, pp.1007 - 1038.

3. Deuteronomy 26,5.

Fragment of cuneiform script, the script used for imperial Aramaic in early times.

The letters were formed by impressions with a pointed stylus on clay tablets. Scholars believe this reveals the origin of the script. It was invented by Accadic or Sumerian tradesmen who imprinted short messages on the clay vessels that contained their merchandise.

Meanwhile Aramaic flourished and spread beyond expectation. When the Assyrians regained control over Mesopotamia (883 - 606 BC), it was not their own language, but Aramaic that gradually became the official language of the empire. Historians ascribe this to the fact that the Aramaic speaking people were good traders, intelligent scribes and excellent organisers. The Assyrians had the practice of dispersing conquered peoples, like the Arameans, throughout their territory. This may effectively have boosted Aramaic as a universal language of communication. The same trend intensified among the Babylonians (606 - 539 BC) and later the Persians (539 - 333 BC). *Imperial Aramaic*, as we call it today, dominated administration, trade, correspondence and diplomacy.

The Old Testament recounts an interesting incident that illustrates the relationship between classical Hebrew and imperial Aramaic. In the year 701 BC the Assyrian king Sennacherib sent an envoy to Jerusalem to demand that Hezekiah surrender the city to his troops. The envoy, who was seated on an elevated platform outside the walls, proclaimed the Assyrian demands in Hebrew.

The Jewish leaders, who were facing him from the city walls, shouted back: 'Please, speak to us in Aramaic, for we understand it. Don't use Hebrew within earshot of the people on the ramparts.'

But he replied: 'Do you think I'm saying this only to you or to the king? Oh no, my message is for the people sitting on the ramparts who, like you, have to eat their own dung and drink their own urine!'[1]

---

1. 2 Kings 18,26-28.

In 701 BC, therefore, only the leaders and not the ordinary people of Jerusalem understood Aramaic. This was to change soon with the ever growing power of Assyria and Babylon. The change came much earlier even for the north, for Galilee and Samaria. Military conquest and the forced migration of peoples gave Aramaic the edge over Hebrew.

Imperial Aramaic was extremely widespread as the *lingua franca*[1] of the whole Middle East for many centuries. Aramaic documents and inscriptions have been found as far south as Egypt, as far north as the Ural Mountains and the Caucasus of Russia, as far east as present-day Afganistan and Pakistan. In Jesus' own province, Galilee, it was the official language from 722 BC, when the Assyrians conquered it, until the end of the Persian rule in 333 BC. Small wonder that it had a great influence on the language of the ordinary people.

Both Hebrew and Aramaic had existed for more than a thousand years before Jesus lived. Both left their mark on Jesus' country.

Hebrew, the 'holy tongue'

What was the language spoken by people in Nazareth when Jesus lived there? Was it Hebrew or Aramaic? The picture that emerges from careful studies is that Hebrew still functioned as a classical and literary language, but that the ordinary people

---

1. A *lingua franca* is a language used for inter-communication by people with different home languages.

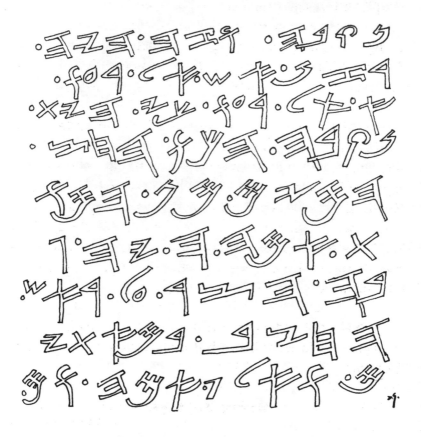

Fragment of the old Hebrew inscription inside the aqueduct of Siloam. It records the moment, in 740 BC, when two parties of stonecutters, starting from both ends of the 1000 ft long tunnel, met in the middle (read 2 Kings 20,20; 2 Chronicles 32,30; Sirach 48,17).

Hebrew adopted alphabetic signs that had been invented by the Phoenicians.

spoke dialects: colloquial Hebrew in Judea, and Galilean Aramaic in Galilee.[1]

Classical Hebrew was no longer a language anyone spoke. But many people still understood it because it was the 'holy language', the language of the Bible. On the sabbath people would hear it read out in the synagogues; and so would remain familiar with it. Hebrew was a prestige language, a language carrying a religious and cultural heritage treasured by the community. It was like the Sanskrit of the Vedas for people in India, or the classical Arabic of the Koran for people who speak modern Arabic dialects.

The situation is described vividly in a rabbinical injunction. 'God says:"You shall teach these commands to your sons". Notice it mentions your sons and not your daughters, says Rabbi Jose ben Akiba. Therefore it has been said: when a young son begins to speak, his father shall talk to him in the Holy Tongue, i.e. Hebrew, and teach him the Law. If the father does not speak to him in the Holy Tongue and teach him the Law, it

---

1. Scholars have argued a lot about the *spoken* language in Jesus' time, - and are still arguing about it. The reasons are easy to understand. The records left in literature or on monuments usually concern the written language, not the spoken one; it is far more difficult to trace the latter. Then, many records which scholars rely upon, are either earlier or later than the first century AD, when Jesus lived. But through wars and movement of populations much changed exactly in that period; so how valid are these records as evidence? Finally, the ancient records themselves refer to Hebrew and Aramaic by conflicting names. See FITZMEYER and RABIN, above, page 77 note 2.

is as if he had buried him'.[1] In other words: classical Hebrew was no longer spoken in families; it was taught as a cultural and religious language.

Hebrew's place as the prestige language is also attested by the practice of the Essenes at Qumran, who were contemporaries of Jesus. Most of their theological treatises were written in Hebrew. It is even possible that Matthew wrote the original version of his Gospel in Hebrew.[2] This would agree well with Matthew's aim to present Jesus' doctrine as a new Law replacing the Old Testament Law.[3] A Hebrew edition of the Gospel for Palestine would make sense since the Rabbis at times employed Hebrew for discussion and teaching.

Jesus himself knew some Hebrew, as is clear from his reading Isaiah 61,1-2 in the synagogue at Nazareth.[4] Did he speak Hebrew when he argued with the scribes: about the meaning of the sabbath rest[5], about divorce,[6] about the washing of hands[7] and similar topics? Personally, I do not think so. It would have

---

1. *Sifre on Deuteronomy 26,4*; see also 11,19. The saying is from the 2nd century AD but reflects a long tradition.

2. J.M.GRINTZ, 'Hebrew as the spoken and written language in the last days of the second Temple', *Journal of Biblical Literature* 179 (1960) pp.32 - 47. The author makes an impressive case for a Hebrew Matthew from internal text analysis. But his overall claims for Hebrew go too far.

3. Matthew 5,1-48.

4. Luke 4,16-19; see above chapter 3, pages 70 - 72.

5. Mark 3,1-6.

6. Matthew 19,3-9.

7. Mark 7,1-13.

been far more natural for him to continue speaking in Galilean Aramaic, the dialect he and his own people were used to. After all, Jesus was a builder, not a scribe; he came from Galilee, not from Judea where rabbinical Hebrew was more common.[1]

Jesus' own language

Without any doubt, Jesus' own language was Aramaic. We know this because the Gospels have preserved some original Aramaic words spoken by Jesus. Some are phrases he employed during his ministry:

'Talitha, qum!' - 'Little girl, get up!'[2]
'Ephphatha!' - 'Be opened!'[3]

Others are spontaneous expressions. When Jesus prays in the garden of Gethsemani, he says: *'Abba* (father, Dad), everything is possible for you. Please, take this cup away from me . . . .'[4] And on the cross he cries out: *'Eli, Eli, lama sabachthani?'*, i.e. 'My God, my God, why have you deserted me?'.[5] These are very personal utterances which Jesus surely made in his own language.

---

1. It is known as 'Mishnaic Hebrew' since part of the later rabbinical teaching of the Mishna was phrased in it.

2. Mark 5,41.

3. Mark 7,34.

4. Mark 14,36; Jesus always employed this Aramaic phrase in his prayer as we can see from later Christian usage: Romans 8,15 and Galatians 4,6.

5. Matthew 27,46; Mark 15,34.

A scroll of Scripture text such as Jesus read from in the synagogue at Nazareth (see Luke 4,16 - 22).
Scrolls were made of pieces of parchment (sheep skin), sewn to each other. Some scrolls reached a length of more than seven meters (21 feet). The reader held the scroll by the handles, unwinding it to the left. Columns and text were read from right to left.

The ordinary people, especially in Galilee, spoke Aramaic - that is, their own brand of it. Since most people could no longer follow classical Hebrew, the custom grew up of giving an Aramaic translation of the Scripture immediately after the text. This was later known as the *targum*. The custom started early. Already in Ezra's time (428 BC ?) the scribes 'read out the Law of God, translating and rendering the sense, so that the people understood what was read'.[1] Usually the reader would improvise the translation, giving a line by line rendering in Aramaic of the Hebrew text. But already in Jesus' time Aramaic targums were written down, as we know from texts preserved at Qumran.[2]

The Galilean Aramaic Jesus spoke, was a mixture of the old 'imperial Aramaic' and colloquial Hebrew. I am sure that Jesus and his contemporaries did not look on it as a foreign language; for them it was simply a form of spoken Hebrew, a dialect, Galilean Hebrew. They did not see it in opposition to their 'holy tongue', classical Hebrew, but as a modern form of it. We can deduce this from the way they speak about their language.

In the Gospel of John we read:

Pilate seated himself on the judgment seat at a place called the Pavement, *in Hebrew* 'Gabbatha'.
John 19,13

---

1. Nehemiah 8,8.

2. The Essenes lived near the Dead Sea at Qumran. They had a great devotion to Scripture. According to one community rule, at least one member of the community should be studying the Bible at any time of day or night. When the Roman armies approached Jerusalem in 70 AD, the Essenes sealed their precious books in clay vessels and hid these in caves. This 'library' was discovered in 1947. A Targum on Job was found in both cave 4 and 9, and a Targum on Leviticus in cave 4.

Fragment of text on the scroll of Isaiah found in Qumran cave 1 (column 44 in document 1QIs[a]). The writing may go back to the second century BC.
This fragment records Isaiah 52,13 - 53,7; that is, the song of the Suffering Servant that meant so much to Jesus: 'Behold, my servant shall prosper. He shall be lifted up and exalted and raised highly . . . .'

Gabbatha clearly responds to the Aramaic word 'gabbeta' (raised place), and not to any Hebrew. An Aramaic expression is, therefore, simply called 'Hebrew' because it was the spoken language of the Jews.

Flavius Josephus tells us that he wrote the original version of his *Jewish Wars* in his 'native tongue' and he repeatedly calls his native tongue 'Hebrew'.[1] But an internal analysis of the work proves the original was written in Aramaic. He tells us the book was written for Parthians, Babylonians, the tribes of Arabia, and for the Jews who live beyond the Euphrates and in Adiabene. These people would only understand Aramaic. Also, for many Jewish religious terms he gives the Aramaic equivalents, not the Hebrew ones.[2] Josephus realised, of course, that classical Hebrew and his own contemporary Aramaic differed. But he saw the one as an extension of the other. Both for him were his native tongue, 'Hebrew'.

We know, therefore, that Jesus spoke Aramaic but that for him, as for his contemporaries, it was just one form of their ancestral tongue, 'Hebrew'. We find this situation even today in many languages: an ancient, classical language co-exists with modern, spoken dialects. The whole complex is considered one language.

Jesus spoke the Galilean version of Aramaic, just like Peter. The Judean servants in the high priest's court recognise him by it. 'You too are from Galilee!', they said to Peter. 'Your speech

1. J.M.GRINTZ, 'Hebrew, etc.'; see above, page 81 note 2.

2. These include: the Pasch, Pentecost, priests, the high priest, sacred linen, etc.

betrays you'.[1]

Jesus, too, must have been recognisable as a Galilean by his speech.

The process of translation

All the present books of the New Testament: the four Gospels, the Acts, the letters of the Apostles and Revelation, have come down to us in Greek. They were written in Greek because that was the international language. The message of Jesus needed to be proclaimed to people throughout the world in the one language they all used as the *lingua franca*.

This means that Jesus' teaching too, though it was in Aramaic originally, has come down to us in a Greek translation. At first, we may feel this as a loss. But then we realise the opposite is true. Translation into many languages was and is needed for Jesus' teaching to reach people in all continents. It is a liberating thought that the Early Church, in spite of its singular respect for Jesus' words, did not want to cling to his original expressions, but insisted that the *meaning* of his words counted more; and that required translation.

As people who read Scripture in depth, we need to acquire a very good understanding of this process of translation which permeates the Gospel.

At the point of origin we always find Jesus' own Aramaic words; words with all the refinements and limitations of any human language. Then we find the translation of these words by the evangelist into a Greek text with characteristically Greek ideas and expressions. Finally we have the formulation of Jesus' message and its meaning in our own language, a formulation

---

1. Matthew 26,73; cf. Mark 14,70; Luke 22,60.

which corresponds to our way of thinking and speaking. It is a dynamic process that should both faithfully reflect the original inspiration and present a creative interpretation for our own time.

To help us understand the process, it is sometimes good to reconstruct the original words of Jesus and see what has happened to them in the course of interpretation.

The 'Our Father'

The original 'Our Father' spoken by Jesus probably had the short form we find with Luke.[1] Let us begin by closely examining the first two phrases:

Father, be sanctified your name.

May come your kingdom.

We notice that in the Greek, as in our literal English translation, the verbs come first. This feels unnatural in English; as it does in Greek. Here we have a clear trace of the original Aramaic text. For in Aramaic, as in all Semitic languages, the verb comes first.

Then, we might well be puzzled by the strange expression: 'May your name be sanctified.' How on earth do we 'sanctify' a 'name'?! It is the kind of thing we would never say in our ordinary speech; nor do we find this kind of expression in Greek. Here again an old Jewish way of speaking shines through. For the Jews the 'name' stands for the person. 'I love your name' means: 'I love you'. The expression 'to sanctify' means: 'to praise, to worship, to acknowledge as holy'.

The overall meaning becomes crystal clear when we discover that this phrase, and the next one, derive from an old Aramaic

---

1. Luke 11,2-4.

prayer, the *Kaddish*, which Jews say even today:
  'Exalted and hallowed be his great Name
  throughout the world which he created
      according to his will.
  May he establish his kingdom
  in your lifetime and in your days and
  in the lifetime of the entire house of Israel
  speedily and soon!'[1]

In this way we discover the Aramaic origin of these two opening lines of the Our Father. The Gospel, though written in Greek, has left us here a rather accurate record of Jesus' *Aramaic* words and thoughts. And we know now what these phrases mean. Jesus wants us to pray, as all Jews did in his time, for the final revelation in this world of God's liberating kingship.

The word 'Father', standing on its own, is exceptional. This is something we never find in Jewish prayer. If 'Father' is used at all, it is qualified by expressions such as 'Our Father', 'Father in heaven', and so on. 'Father' reveals Jesus' personal and intimate relationship to God. It reminds us of Jesus' own Aramaic term: *Abba*.[2]

1. *Siddur Tehillat Hashem*, New York 1982, p.42; here in its earliest form, cf. I.ELBOGEN, *Der jüdische Gottesdienst in seiner geschichtlichen Entwicklung*, Hildesheim 1962, pp.92 - 98.

2. Mark 14,36; more on this in my WALKING ON WATER book *God is close*. See also J.JEREMIAS, *Abba. Studien zur neutestamentlichen Theologie und Zeitgeschichte*, Göttingen 1966, pp. 15 - 67.

Scholars have reconstructed the Our Father in Aramaic. This is what it sounded like in Jesus' own words:

Abba!
Father!
Yitqaddash   shemâk.
May be sanctified name yours.

Têtê   malkûtâk.
May come   kingdom yours.

Lachmân   de limchâr /
Bread ours of tomorrow[1]
  hab   lân   yômâ dên
  give to us day   this.

û   shebôq lân   chôbênan
and forgive to us debts[2] ours
    kedi   shebaqnân le chayyâbênan.
    as herewith forgive we to debtors ours.

we   lâ   ta'êlinnan   le nisyôn.
and not let fall us   into trial.[3]

---

1. The 'bread of tomorrow'; like the Jews gathered in the desert (Exodus 16,4-5). It implies the future bread brought by the Messiah; also the bread needed from day to day, as we find in the Greek translation (Luke 11,3).

2. Jews understood that 'debts' here means 'sins'; Luke translates it as 'sins' for his non-Jewish readers (Luke 11,4).

3. For the reconstruction and a good explanation, see J.JERE MIAS, *New Testament Theology*, London 1981, pp.193 - 203.

Matthew, who wrote a Gospel for the Jews in Palestine and who probably composed it in classical Hebrew, has his own version of the Our Father.[1] In this literal translation of the Greek text I have printed in italics what Matthew has changed or added:

> Father *ours who (is) in the heavens,*
> may be sanctified name yours!
> May come kingdom yours!
> *May be done will yours*
>   *as in heaven so on earth.*
> Bread ours of the day
>   give to us today.
> And forgive to us debts ours,
>   as also we have forgiven debtors ours.
> And not let fall us into trial,
>   *but deliver us from evil.*

Matthew's three additions can be well understood by the purpose of his Gospel. Since he was writing for Jews, he defines the invocation 'Father' with the addition: 'who art in heaven'. This is how Jews would pray. Matthew knew that Jesus called God simply *Abba*, 'Dad'. But here he is teaching the prayer to us.

Then he had to explain what Jesus meant by the coming of the kingdom. Jesus was not praying for a nationalistic, political restoration of Israel, but for a kingdom of moral values. That is why he adds what the kingdom means: that the Father's will be done on earth as in heaven.

Jesus' petition : 'Do not let us fall into trial' was also open to misunderstanding. It did not mean that Jesus wants us to pray to

---

1. Matthew 6,9-13.

be saved from suffering or pain; it means, as Matthew explains, that we should pray to be saved from sin, from doing anything wrong. We see Matthew doing here what the evangelists do throughout their writing. They act as 'dynamic' interpreters of Jesus' words; often giving *the sense* of what he said rather than just a 'dead', word-for-word rendering.

For the sake of comparison I will print here a reconstruction of what Matthew's *Hebrew* version of the Our Father looked like, next to the Aramaic original. It is not difficult to see how close the old, classical text (Hebrew) is to the dialect (Aramaic) which Jesus spoke.[1]

ARAMAIC	HEBREW
Abba!	**Abbênû** *she beshamâyim.*
Yitqaddash shemâk.	**Yitqaddash shemâk.**
Têtê malkûtâk.	**Tabô malkûtâk.**
	Yu'ashah rissônekâ
	ka'asher beshamâyim kên bâ'âress.
Lachmân delimchâr	**Et-lachem hayyôm**
hab lân yômâ dên.	**ten lanû hayyôm.**
û Shebôq lân chôbênan	**û Selach lanû et-chabôtênû**
kedi shebaqnân	**ka'asher selachnû gam anachnû**
lechayyâbênan.	**lechêbênû.**
We lâ ta'êlinnan le nisyôn.	**We al-tabînû lêdê nisyôn**
	kî im chalassnû min harra'.

---

1. This Hebrew reconstruction of Matthew 6,9-13 is based on *Habbeshûrah Haqqedôshah Mattai*, ed.J.M.BAUCHET, Jerusalem 1948, pp.16 - 17.

QUESTIONS FOR PERSONAL STUDY

1. Matthew gives us this incident from Jesus' passion:

> **Jesus cried out in a loud voice: *'Eli, Eli, lama sabachthani?'*, that is: 'My God, my God, why have you deserted me?'**
> **Some of the bystanders said: 'He's calling on Elijah!', and one of them quickly went to get a sponge and dip it in vinegar. Putting it on a stick, he gave Jesus to drink.**
> **'Let us see', the others said, 'whether Elijah will come to save him!'**
>
> *Matthew 27,46-49*

Did they really think Jesus was calling on Elijah?

2. The Gospel of Mark has preserved two unusual, Aramaic words of Jesus: *Talitha, kum!* (Mark 5,41) and *Ephphatha* (Mark 7,34).
What would be Mark's interest in the original Aramaic here?

3. Please, comment on these instructions of Vatican II:

> **Easy access to sacred Scripture should be provided for all Christian believers . . . .**
> **With motherly concern the Church sees to it that readable and accurate translations be produced in different languages. These translations should be based on the original texts of the sacred books.'**
>
> *Divine Revelation*, no 22.

Space for your own notes

THE LIMITS OF LANGUAGE

Every language has its own possibilities and limitations. What we can say in one language we cannot say so easily in another. We have to interpret what a person says according to the language that person speaks. This applies also to Jesus. In this chapter we will explore the far reaching implications of this important truth.

No one familiar with today's world can have missed the phenomenon of 'fundamentalism'. There are fundamentalist Muslims and fundamentalist Christians. What does the term mean? In a nutshell, fundamentalists are convinced that a particular religion should be rigidly maintained in the shape of its original foundation. The original expressions of doctrine, religious practice and moral code are considered immutable. Fundamentalism denies the legitimacy of change. Things have to remain always the same.

Fundamentalist Muslims, for example, will not accept the equality of women. Women have to wear a veil in public, are subject to their husbands, can be divorced easily, must share a harem with other wives. In fundamentalist views their position can never change because it has been fixed once for all in verses of the inspired book, the *Koran*, and in tradition, the *hadîth*. As things were at the time of Mohammed, they have to be for ever because this is 'the will of *Allah*'.

Christian fundamentalists take a similar stance; the only difference being that now it is the Bible and Christian tradition that reveal the immutable will of God. Sociologists maintain that the roots of today's fundamentalism have less to do with one's religion than with social and psychological needs: the fear of change, escape into authoritarian structures, a refusal to face up to complex new challenges. But the religious angle remains a factor. Fundamentalist Christians believe they are the only ones who are faithful to the original Gospel.

Fidelity to Jesus' words

I find there is a lot of confusion about this even among more balanced believers. Somehow they feel uneasy about the changes introduced by their Church community, such as the reforms sanctioned for the Catholic Church by Vatican II. Changes are looked upon as a climb down, a compromise with 'the world', a lowering of standards. Some Catholics frantically cling to their Latin Mass or to communion on the tongue; or feel a married clergy would betray the 'sanctity' of the priest-hood. The misconceptions on which such feelings rest range from mere ignorance to absurd illusions.

I remember one old religious sister in Holland who told me she would never receive communion on the hand because Jesus himself gave it to his apostles on the tongue! She had picked up this misinformation from a leaflet which stated that this is how St.Brigitte of Sweden, in a vision, had seen Jesus distribute communion at the Last Supper. I saw a copy of the leaflet. In a drawing it showed Jesus, vested in a chasuble and holding a modern chalice, distributing consecrated hosts to the apostles who devoutly knelt before him, holding out their tongues. The historical truth is, of course, that Jesus never wore a chasuble, nor owned a chalice, nor used white round hosts, nor gave communion on the tongue. The example may seem farfetched, but experience shows that even relatively well educated people may retain some rather simplistic ideas of how Jesus revealed the Father to us.

Faithfulness *is* of the essence. We have to remain faithful to Jesus' original vision, to what he revealed to us about God, to his principles, to the community of believers which he began. But this faithfulness itself requires openness to change. Jesus never intended to leave a ready-made product; he sowed a seed that would need to grow. Or, to put it in its biblical context, he spoke words that needed refinement and interpretation. If we, Catholics, want to be faithful to Jesus we have to listen to the new dynamic interpretation given to his words by the Church in the Second Vatican Council. And, guided by the Council, we ourselves should interpret Jesus' words dynamically in new ways responding to our own situation.

Fundamentalists are almost without exception literalists. They think that the whole meaning of Christianity is contained in verses of the New Testament that define everything word for word. They believe that Jesus, and his apostles, said everything that could be said, once and for all. The Gospel is closed. Just read it word for word and you know what is in it and what not. They forget that Jesus spoke a *human* language which, of necessity, was time-bound and limited. Moreover, he never wanted to speak a closed message; he spoke a living word.

Exploring language

Jesus spoke and thought in Aramaic. But if his words are also spoken *to us*, as we Christians believe, they need to be given a fresh and wider interpretation. We live in a world of new realities and new thoughts. What Jesus said can only affect us if our own thought and our own situation is taken into account.

ΤΡωΠΙCΤΟΙΟγΚΕ
ΓΕΝΕCΘΑΙΤΟγΜΕ
ΤΕΡΟΝΤΙCΔωCΕΙ
γΜΙΝ
ΟγΔΕΙCΟΙΚΕΤΗCΔγ
ΝΑΤΑΙΔγCΙΚγΡΙΟΙ·
ΔΟγΛΕγΕΙΝΕΙΓΑΡ
ΤΟΝΕΝΑΜΙCΗCΙ
ΚΑΙΤΟΝΕΤΕΡΟΝΑ
ΓΑΤΤΗCΕΙΗΕΡΟC
ΑΝΘΕΞΕΤΑΙΚΑΤγ
ΕΤΕΡΟγΚΑΤΑΦΡΟ
ΝΗCΕΙΟγΔγΝΑCΘΝ
Θ͞ωΔΟγΛΕγΕΙΝΚΛ
ΜΑΜωΝΑ
ΗΚΟγΟΝΔΕΤΑγΤΑ

Handing on the text of Scripture has always been part of Christian tradition. This fragment, from the Codex Sinaiticus (4th century AD) shows how the Greek text was transmitted at the time. All letters were in square capitals. There were no spaces between the words, neither were there punctuation marks. The text speaks of the rite of atonement (Leviticus 16).

Let us start with some simple examples of linguistic disparity with which we may already be familiar. In Aramaic, people would often use the expression *'to be called* something' when they meant *'to be* something'. They might say: 'I am called a British citizen', where we would say: 'I am a British citizen.' All of us will recognise these phrases from the Gospel:

* **They will be called children of God.**[1]
* **He will be called the least in heaven.**[2]
* **My house shall be called a house of prayer.**[3]
* **He shall be called Son of the Most High.**[4]
* **I am not worthy to be called your son.**[5]

Not only does the expression sound awkward in today's English, it could even be understood wrongly. In our way of speaking, the fact that something is *called* this or that, does not mean it *is* that reality. And yet, that is what it means in Aramaic. God did not want his Temple *to be called* a house of prayer. He wanted it *to be* a house of prayer.

Or consider the way Aramaic uses nouns. Often a noun appears where we would use an adjective. In stead of speaking of 'a filthy dog', Jesus' contemporaries would say 'a dog *of filth*'. A 'beautiful ring' is expressed as 'a ring *of beauty*', 'a strong soldier' as 'a soldier *of strength*'. The Aramaic term 'the God of mercy' means in our language 'the merciful God'.

---

1. Matthew 5,9.

2. Matthew 5,19.

3. Matthew 21,13.

4. Luke 1,32.

5. Luke 15,19.

Compare these phrases from the Gospel:

      * **commandments of men** = human commandments;[1]
      * **the steward of iniquity** = the dishonest steward;[2]
      * **the mammon of iniquity** = evil money;[3]
      * **the Spirit of truth** = the truthful Spirit;[4]
      * **the wisdom of the just** = saintly wisdom;[5]
      * **people of pleasure** = people with whom
                           God is pleased;[6]
      * **words of grace** = gracious words.[7]

Every language has its own list of linking-up words. In Aramaic the expression 'son of . . . .' can indicate a man with any type of relationship. The plural 'sons of . . . .' includes women. Practically each case has to be examined on its own merit.

      * **a son of peace** = a peaceful man;[8]

---

1. Matthew 15,9: 'They teach commandments of men'.

2. Luke 16,8: 'The master praised the steward of iniquity'.

3. Luke 16,9: 'Use the mammon of iniquity to make you friends'.

4. John 14,17: 'The Father will give you the Spirit of truth'.

5. Luke 1,17: 'He will turn the disobedient back to the wisdom of the just'.

6. Luke 2,14: 'Glory to God on high and on earth peace to people of pleasure'.

7. Luke 4,22: 'They were amazed at the words of grace that came from his lips'.

8. Luke 10,6:'If a son of peace lives there, your peace will rest on him'.

* **sons of thunder** = impetuous people;[1]
* **the sons of this world** = worldly people;[2]
* **the son of perdition** = the man who risks damnation;[3]
* **the sons of the evil one** = devilish, wicked people;[4]
* **sons of the bride chamber** = wedding guests;[5]
* **sons of the resurrection** = people who have been raised.[6]

It is clear from these examples that a literal translation is not necessarily the best translation. In fact, in quite a number of cases literalists miss the real meaning of what Jesus wanted to say. It is not what the words sound like in English that matters, but what they conveyed in Aramaic. And that brings us to the question of thought.

---

1. Mark 3,17: 'James the son of Zebedee and James' brother John to whom he gave the name *Boanerges*, that is *Sons of Thunder*'.

2. Luke 16.8: 'The sons of this world are more astute with their own people than are the sons of light'.

3. John 17,12: 'I have lost no one except the son of perdition'.

4. Matthew 13,38: 'The good seed are the sons of the Kingdom, the weeds are the sons of the evil one'.

5. Matthew 9,15: 'The sons of the bride chamber cannot mourn as long as the bridegroom is with them'.

6. Luke 2,36: 'They can no longer die, for they are like angels and sons of God, being sons of the resurrection'.

This fragment (from the Codex Chisianus, 1000 AD?) illustrates how the writing of Greek had changed over the centuries. The letters are now rounded (cursive). Upper and lower case are distinct. Words are spaced and punctuation marks have been introduced.

The text records Daniel 12,11-12 which announces the 'disastrous abomination' that will be erected in the Temple. Jesus quotes this text in the Gospel (Mark 13,14).

Ways of thinking

We do not just speak in our language. We think in it. Our language defines our concepts and to a great extent limits them. This is of great importance in our studying of Jesus' words. It implies that sometimes we have to refine the expressions used in the Gospel to come to a balanced understanding.

Aramaic, like its sister language Hebrew, could not easily express degrees, such as more or less. It could say a man was tall or short. It did not possess a comparative case (taller/shorter) or a superlative case (the tallest/shortest). To say 'John is the tallest in his group', Aramaic came no further than saying: 'John is tall among his group'. That is why **'Blessed are you among women'** should be translated by us as: 'You are the most blessed of women'.[1] **'Mary has chosen the good part'** means 'Mary has chosen the better part'.[2]

This lack of nuance can be seen clearly in the handling of the term *hate*. Jesus, we are told by Luke, spoke these uncompromising words:

> **'If anyone does not hate his father, mother, wife, children, brothers and sisters, he cannot be my disciple.'**[3]

Hating here means 'loving less'.

---

1. Luke 1,42.

2. Luke 10,42.

3. Luke 14,26.

The Greek version of Matthew rightly translates:

'Who loves father and mother more than me is not worthy of me'.[1]

However, it is useful to reflect on the fact that Jesus *did* use the expression 'hating'. When he left his own family and kinsfolk in Nazareth, as we saw in chapter three, he must have experienced this as a need of 'hating' them for the sake of his Father. Was the tribe of Levi not praised in the Old Testament for turning against their own relatives for God's sake?

He says of his father and mother,

'I have not seen them'.

His brothers he does not know,

nor does he acknowledge his children.[2]

The point is that in Jesus' thinking there was a sharp divide between for and against.

'Who is not for me is against me'.[3]

This tendency, which is so typically Aramaic, also shows itself in expressions such as:

* **I want mercy not sacrifice.**[4]

* **It is harder for a rich man to enter the kingdom of heaven than for a camel to go through the eye of a needle!**[5]

* **If your right eye makes you sin, rip it out and throw**

---

1. Matthew 10,37.

2. Deuteronomy 33,9; cf. Exodus 32,25-29.

3. Matthew 12,30; see also Luke 9,40!

4. Matthew 9,13.

5. Mark 10,25.

it away. It is better for you to lose one member than to have your whole body thrown into hell![1]

Such statements are deliberate exaggerations to express a principle strongly. Although they sound like absolutes, they are not meant to be. Jesus knew full well they would need refinement, both in expression and application. Without presumption we can say that many things that are stated in the Gospel needed to be re-stated by later generations of Christians with more 'nuance' in the light of further reflection and experience.

This may sound scandalous to some people because they may not have realised that this is implied in incarnation. If Jesus was truly human in everything except sin,[2] he was limited too in the range of what he could think and what he could say. Jesus proclaimed principles which he presented as absolutes. It is up to us, today's Church, to refine these within the context of our own lives.

Take the example of divorce. With characteristic forthrightness Jesus denounced it, on principle.

>   * **Human beings must not separate what God has joined together!**[3]
>   * **A man who divorces his wife and marries another woman commits adultery.**
>   **And a woman who divorces her husband and marries another man commits adultery.**[4]

---

1. Matthew 5,29.

2. Hebrews 4,15.

3. Mark 10,9.

4. Mark 10,11-12.

In Jesus' time animal skins were used to keep water, but also wine. If wine was still fermenting, it stretched the skin.

Jesus bases a small parable on this fact. 'People do not put new wine into old skins. If they do, the skins burst, the wine leaks out and the skins are ruined. No, they put new wine into fresh skins to preserve both' (Matthew 9,17).

For Jesus this illustrated that his actions should not be judged by Old Testament norms. Would he not agree wholeheartedly that the same applies to every succeeding generation that finds itself in new circumstances?

If we take this literally, as some Christians have done, divorce would never be allowed.

However, already in apostolic times the Church formulated refinements and exceptions. The community for which Matthew's Gospel was written accepted unfaithfulness as a reason for divorce.[1] Paul decided that converts could divorce if their non-Christian partner demanded this.[2] Throughout the centuries the Church has dissolved marriages for pastoral reasons: when the partners had not consummated their marriage, when one of them wanted to enter a monastery, or when a polygamous man became a Christian.[3] All such cases Jesus did not foresee and could not foresee.

The growth of doctrine

At the Council of Nicaea in 325 AD the Arians refused to accept the new creed which had been drawn up. They objected to the fact that God the Son is called *consubstantial* (= 'of the same divine nature') as the Father. This word, they said, could not be found in the Gospels. Therefore, it had no validity. By insisting on its use the Church acknowledged a crucial principle, namely that our faith can be and should be expressed in new theological terms relevant to our own time.[4]

---

1. Matthew 5,32; 19,9.

2. 1 Corinthians 7,15.

3. J.WIJNGAARDS, 'Do Jesus' words on divorce (Lk 16,18) admit of no exception?', *Jeevadhara* 30 (1975) pp. 399 - 411.

4. A classic about this is *Essay on the Development of Christian Doctrine* by Cardinal John Henry NEWMAN; re-published by Penguin in 1974, ed. J.M.CAMERON.

Many things that Jesus said or did needed to be refined in further theological discussion. Jesus brought people together in a new community. He himself never used the term 'Church' for this community. The term 'church', *ekklêsia*, was a vital refinement and development in the thinking of the Greek-speaking converts in Syria and Asia Minor.[1] The same applies to many other terms such as 'elder', 'bishop', 'deacon' and 'priest'; they do not go back to Jesus but to the Early Christian communities.[2]

The ordination of women has become an important issue for many Christian Churches. Obviously, the question has arisen in our own time because of our own contemporary context: awareness of women's rights, the shortage of male ministers in some countries and pastoral opportunities for women priests. Many arguments have been brought forward, for and against. One of them, which I consider totally invalid, is the contention that Christ deliberately *excluded* women from the ministry. This momentous decision, attributed to Christ, is not based on any firm Gospel evidence, but on the circumstance that we find no women among the twelve apostles Jesus chose. The argument simply overlooks the fact that Jesus acted within the culture of the time, and at that time religious leadership was exercised by

1. Read more about this in the WALKING ON WATER book *Gospel and Community*. The word 'church' in Matthew 18,17 is an addition by the evangelist.

2. E.SCHILLEBEECKX, *Ministry, and a case for change*, London 1981. The author offers a historical analysis of how the ministries developed and draws conclusions as to the reforms in ministry the present-day Church could and should make.

men.[1] How could it ever mean a ban on women's participation in the ministry decreed by Christ for all generations to come?

Or consider the word *sacrament*. It is a Latin term introduced by theologians such as St.Augustine and St.Ambrose. For them it designated any religious rite. Augustine, for example, considered the blessing of a house and the foot washing on Maunday Thursday to be 'sacraments'. Only in the Middle Ages did the term acquire the exact theological precision with which we employ it today. Baptism, imposition of hands, forgiveness of sins, the Eucharistic meal: we find them in the Gospels in embryo, as a seed. The later pastoral practice of the Church and the theological thinking that goes with it, are further developments which were not and could not be foreseen by Jesus.

There is nothing degrading in such a statement. It is not as if by it we were to deny Jesus' pre-eminence or tarnish his glory as 'the exact likeness of God's being'.[2] Nothing of the sort.

Jesus limited himself deliberately to what he could think and say from within his own Aramaic experience. By doing so he truly showed himself one of us. And he entrusted to his apostles and all future generations of Christians the task of developing and refining the truths and principles he had enunciated. He did not make us servants, but successors. 'You will do greater things than I have done, because I am going to the Father'.[3] To

1. J.WIJNGAARDS, *Did Christ rule out women priests?*, McCrimmon's, Great Wakering 1986.

2. Hebrews 1,3.

3. John 14,12.

accomplish this task, Jesus left us his own Spirit who would lead us 'to the fullness of the Truth'.[1]

Peace and justice

The limitation of Jesus' thinking also extended to social issues. I do not doubt for a moment that Jesus, who sided with the poor as we will see in future chapters, strongly believed in the fundamental equality of all human beings. That equality was one of the pillars of God's kingdom. But he did not and could not foresee all the implications as we do today.

Slavery, for example, was a reality in Jesus' days. Jesus accepted it as such. He refers to it in his parables; as when he says we should be like good slaves who faithfully care for their master's property until he returns.[2] The fidelity of a good slave impressed Jesus.

If one of you has a slave who is ploughing or minding sheep, will you say to him when he returns from the field: 'Come and have your meal immediately?'
Would he not more likely say: 'Get my supper ready. Make yourself tidy and wait on me while I eat and drink; after that you yourself can have your meal'? Must he be grateful to his slave for doing as he was told?

---

1. John 14,17; 14,25-26; 16,12-15. This is more fully worked out in J.WIJNGAARDS, *Inheriting the Master's Cloak*, Ave Maria Press, Notre Dame 1976, pp. 151 - 157; *The Gospel of John and his Letters*, Michael Glazier, Wilmington 1986, pp. 222 - 233.

2. Luke 12,42-48.

**The same applies to you: when you have done all you
have been told to, say, 'We're only slaves; we've done
no more than our duty'.[1]**

It is crystal clear from Jesus' way of talking that he had not
drawn the radical conclusion that slavery should be abolished.
He stayed within the thinking of his own Aramaic society.
Concepts like 'equality for all', basic human rights, eradicating
discrimination, did not exist in his vocabulary. All this in spite of
the fact, as I will show later, that he had initiated the process
that would lead to such radical notions.

Jesus' acceptance of slavery misled some Church leaders and
theologians as late as in 1866 to declare that slavery is allowed
by God.[2] What they forgot is that Jesus himself could not and
would not draw all the conclusions and implications contained
in his vision.

Jesus could not and did not foresee all the implications his
principles would have for eradicating racial discrimination, for
supporting the United Nations, for preserving our ecology, for a
just economic order, for sound relations between employers

---

1. Luke 17,7-10

2. The Holy Office declared in 1866: 'Slavery itself, considered
as such in its essential nature, is not at all contrary to the natural
and divine law, and there can be several just titles of slavery and
these are referred to by approved theologians and commenta-
tors of the sacred canons . . . . It is not contrary to the natural
and divine law for a slave to be sold, bought, exchanged or
given.'
Read: J.F.MAXWELL, 'The Development of Catholic Doctrine
concerning Slavery', *World Jurist* 11 (1969-70) pp.147-192; 291-
324.

Figs, together with olives, grapes and wheat, formed the main source of wealth for farmers in Galilee. We are not surprised that figs figure in many of Jesus' images (read Mark 11,12 - 25; Luke 13,6 - 9).

The fig tree also provided one of Jesus' images concerning 'the signs of the times'. 'Take the fig tree as a parable. When its twigs grow supple and leaves bud forth, you know summer is near' (Matthew 24,32). Every generation of Christians should read the signs of its own time.

and employees, and a thousand other developments that will help to make our earth habitable for all. Jesus never thought of these things; but given his principles we know he would support them if he could think and speak in today's language.

The same applies to 'democracy' in the Church. Although the Church is not a democracy in the sense that authority derives from God and not from the people, decision-making processes in the Church can follow a democratic pattern, in line with our present-day world. In fact, this is what has now been strongly promoted by the reforms of Vatican II. It can be seen in new procedures for electing the Pope, and bishops; in co-responsibility at international, diocesan and parish levels; in financial accountability; in the new role attributed to lay people in almost every activity of the Church. The seeds for this lie in the Gospel, its realisation is a task of Jesus' followers today.

Paradoxically, by speaking a limited language, Jesus gave his universal message an almost unlimited scope. The working out of what he said is *our* job, a job for each and every Christian; and of all of us together in the Church. It is an inspiring challenge that should fill us with awe and courage.

QUESTIONS FOR PERSONAL STUDY

1. Jesus demanded a complete acceptance of his message. He stated:

> **'Heaven and earth shall pass away, but my words shall not pass away'**
>
> *Matthew 24,35*

Does this not mean his teaching has to be taken literally as 'the last word' on every question?

2. What are the full implications of this parable?

> **'The kingdom of heaven is like a woman who takes some yeast and mixes it with forty kilograms of flour until the whole batch of dough rises.'**
>
> *Matthew 13,33; see also Matthew 13,31-32*

3. Vatican II states unequivocally:

> **'Every type of discrimination, whether social or cultural, whether based on sex, race, colour, social status, language or religion, is to be overcome and eradicated as contrary to God's will . . . .**
>
> **People should spare no effort to banish every trace of slavery, whether social or political . . . .'**
>
> *The Church in the Modern World*, no 2

Do Jesus' words fall short of this ideal? How to reconcile a statement such as:

> **'No slave is greater than his master.'**
>
> *Matthew 10,24*

114

LANGUAGE THAT LIBERATES.

Jesus came from the country side, as we have seen. He spoke the language of the ordinary people in Galilee. He did not address his message only to the learned or to the religious upper classes. He spoke to the many people in the towns and villages of Galilee who needed liberation. Did he succeed as a spiritual teacher? Did his words set people free or make them more dependent?

To explain the meaning of this question, let me introduce someone from the northeast of Brazil, a man called Paolo Freire.[1] Freire who was born in Recife in 1921, resembles Jesus in some respects. His parents were middle-class people who had suffered great hardships on account of the economic depression. As a boy Paolo often went to school on an empty stomach. His clothes were second hand. The family could not afford to pay for textbooks. As an adolescent, Paolo turned away from the Church for a while because of its lack of involvement in people's every-day struggles. Fortunately he rediscovered his Christian faith and he decided to dedicate his life to helping the poor.

Education, Freire saw, was essential. But the official school system did not liberate people, it enslaved them. How to describe the situation at the time? A small elite of powerful fami-

---

1. Among various biographies written about Freire I recommend: D.COLLINS, *Paulo Freire. His life, works and thought*, New York 1977.

lies owned all the land, ran the factories, controlled trade and held on to political posts. The rural population and the working class who lived in dire misery were exploited, to produce more wealth for the lucky few at the top.[1] What did the schools do in this situation? Freire found that instead of helping the poor to become real persons - individuals who can think and act for themselves, schools tightened people's bonds even more.

Textbooks did little more than instil into the minds of pupils the notions and values that would uphold the prevailing system. Students were taught reading and writing, maths, geography, history and religion, in such a way that they would become more useful employees, submissive citizens and naive consumers. Parcels of knowledge were passed on which the students had patiently to receive, memorise and repeat. Freire compared this form of education to 'banking'. People are treated as objects. Knowledge is 'deposited' in them as an investment which will yield financial profit in the end.

The result of this kind of education is that people always remain dependent.[2] They cannot grow as individuals. They do not learn to stand on their own feet as people who share responsibility for their world. To achieve this true personal growth Freire developed a new form of education which he successfully launched among the rural populations of Brazil and

---

1. E.DEKADT, *Catholic Radicals in Brazil*, Oxford 1970.

2. 'The acceptance of the values of the rich is the greatest obstacle for the liberation of the poor.' J.MOLTMANN, *The Way of Jesus Christ*, London 1989, p. 101.

Chile.[1] Freire coined the phrase 'conscientisation'.[2] His insights and methods have revolutionised education all over the world, and have greatly influenced ordinary school curriculums as well as adult literacy programmes.

You may well wonder why I introduce Freire's thought here while we are talking about Jesus. The answer is that Freire has focussed attention on right and wrong forms of teaching. He has also proved beyond doubt that language plays a key role in such teaching. Since we believe that Jesus is the greatest teacher of all times, the question arises: how does he fit in?

Bad teachers impose their ideas in ready-made form. They consider themselves omniscient, the students as ignorant. They talk, expecting the students to listen and memorise. They reduce the students to being recipients; passive objects; parrots; robots. They cast themselves in the role of the potter who can mould the clay to any form he likes. Bad teachers enslave people. Good teachers, however, impart knowledge in such a way that they encourage students to think for themselves. Teaching is dialogue, communication, a shared search. Good teachers set people free because they allow them to grow as autonomous, free individuals.

----

1. P.FREIRE, 'Education as the Practice of Freedom' and 'Extension or Communication' both published under the collective title: *Education for Critical Consciousness*, New York 1973; *Pedagogy of the Oppressed*, New York 1972; 'The Educational Role of the Churches in Latin America', *Latin American Documentation* (LADOC), vol.3, no 14 (1972) pp. 1 - 14.

2. P.Freire explains the term well in 'Conscientisation', *The Month*, May 1974, pp. 575 - 578; see also *The Outlook* 14 (1975) pp. 219 - 224.

The Old Testament frequently uses the image of the potter. Remembering how God 'moulded Adam from clay' (Genesis 29,16), prophets point to this image to demonstrate our total dependence on God (Isaiah 29,16; 45,9; 64,7). However, the image did not exclude, rather presupposed, our human free will (see Jeremiah 18,1-6; Sirach 15,11-20).

Why did Jesus not use the image of the potter? Did he detect its connotations of rigidity and passivity? It is certainly interesting that to denote people he preferred living images, such as a seeds, plants and trees.

May we not, without realising what we are doing, push Jesus into the role of a *very bad* teacher? Jesus, we might think, knew everything and, while on earth, formulated a set of revealed truths that he handed over to us. This ready-made 'deposit of faith' contains the articles of doctrine and principles of morality that have been laid down once for all. As Jesus' students we have faithfully to believe and obey, transmit and execute what he has told us. What, in such a fundamentalist mind set, we do not realise is that this conception reduces us, believers, to being passive 'objects' and chains us for good to rigid forms of belief and action.

But was this Jesus' way of teaching? Yes, Jesus *did* reveal God's loving intentions. There *are* truths and principles which belong to a 'deposit of faith'. But did Jesus share this revelation in such a way as to enslave us; or to set us free? Did he silence us once for all; or did he want us to think for ourselves too? Did he lay down rigid models of behaviour; or did he expect us to make responsible decisions for ourselves?

Paolo Freire has suggested some useful norms to judge teachers by.[1] In particular, I am impressed by three practical rules to help us evaluate a teacher's *use of language*.

1. What kind of things does the teacher speak about? Does he use words that alienate his pupils? Or do his words start from the experience of his pupils and generate discussion?

2. Does the teacher speak down to his students? Or does he help them to think for themselves?

3. Does the teacher begin a process of challenging systems and structures that need to be changed?

---

1. It is not my intention to report fully on Freire's method or endorse it in every respect. I select those norms that seem relevant to me in the context of the Gospel.

I want to take these questions as our starting point for a fresh look at Jesus' language. Jesus spoke as a teacher. Does his message liberate us? Does it make us critical, conscious and responsible Christians?

The choice of words

Freire discovered that we dominate thought by *the words* we choose. Textbooks that speak about presidents, prime ministers and generals make everyday life insignificant. Advertisers promote consumer needs by speaking of their products. Preachers may narrow people's outlook by mouthing religious jargon unrelated to down-to-earth reality. For his adult literacy campaigns Freire studied the life of the ordinary people and carefully selected 'generative words': words taken from their situation that could generate critical reflection. For the rural workers of Pernambuco, these were: shack, plough, well, hunger, and so on. A word was illustrated with a drawing that presented the web of relationships involved in the word. Each word became the core of a lesson that made people reflect on their world.

What about Jesus? What words did he use?

The Gospels show that almost all his teachings are phrased in images taken from people's every-day lives. We take it so much for granted that we may not sufficiently realise the implications of this momentous fact. If Jesus truly was the one who revealed God to us through his own human personality, as we truly believe, he brought this revelation in the words and images of ordinary people. He did not speak as a lecturer at the University, or as a learned theologian. He used words and images familiar to Galilean country folk.

Many of Jesus' sayings reflect knowledge of a farmer's life. He speaks of sowing the seed,[1] weeding,[2] reaping the harvest.[3] He knows a farmer needs to keep his hand on the plough while ploughing,[4] that birds eat seeds,[5] that thorn bushes strangle the young shoots,[6] that landlords demand their portion of the crop.[7] He describes the care lavished on single fig trees,[8] the pruning required by vines[9] and the mysterious growth of the mustard tree.[10] He talks of a farmer laying a yoke on an ox and a burden on a donkey,[11] or taking the animals to a well to drink.[12] This is the kind of life people knew. It was the day-to-day reality they were exposed to.

Jesus also takes his images from the life of shepherds, soldiers, tax collectors, landowners, merchants, fishermen, the blind, kings and generals as seen by ordinary people.

---

1. Mark 4,3-9.

2. Matthew 13,24-30.

3. John 4,35-38.

4. Luke 9,62.

5. Mark 4,4.

6. Mark 4,7.

7. Mark 12,2.

8. Luke 13,6-9.

9. John 15,1-2.

10. Mark 4,30-32.

11. Matthew 11,29-30.

12. Luke 13,15.

He points to things people had observed in nature: the enchanting flowers of the field that appear after the first rains,[1] the vultures that descend on the corpse of an animal,[2] the dark red sky that announces rain,[3] the beautiful sunrises over the lake of Galilee[4] and towns built on a hill that can be seen from afar.[5]

Jesus often relates his teaching to what people experienced at home. A house built on sand is not safe; only a house built on rock will survive a storm.[6] A woman who has lost a coin will sweep the whole floor carefully till she finds it.[7] In the evening people will light an oil lamp. It is not put under a bowl but on a stand so that it can give light to the entire room.[8] Meat and fish will soon rot if they are not salted.[9] A man who goes to sleep at night will not easily get up when someone knocks on the door to borrow a loaf of bread; for his wife and children are sleeping on mattresses around him all over the floor.[10]

---

1. Matthew 6,28-30.

2. Luke 17,37.

3. Matthew 16,3.

4. Matthew 5,45.

5. Matthew 5,14.

6. Luke 6,46-49.

7. Luke 15,8-10.

8. Matthew 5,16.

9. Matthew 5,13.

10. Luke 11,5-8.

The details of a woman's life did not escape Jesus' observant eye. What is particularly interesting is that he often pairs examples taken from a man's world with matching ones from a woman's. As a good teacher he had not forgotten that there were women among his audience.

The parable of the shepherd looking for the lost sheep is followed by the parable of the woman searching for her lost coin (Luke 15,4-10). The kingdom of God is like the mustard seed planted by a farmer and yeast mixed in dough by a woman (Matthew 13,31-33). The image of the man wanting bread at night is matched by the widow pestering the judge (Luke 11,5-8 and 18,1-8).

When the last day comes, 'of two men working in the field, one will be taken (to heaven), one left; of two women grinding corn at the millstone, one will be taken, one left' (Matthew 24,41).

Jesus mentions everyday objects: the heavy millstone turned by two women to grind corn[1], an old coat patched with pieces of new cloth[2], skins used to keep wine[3], the seasoning herbs, mint, dill and cumin[4], a sieve used to strain a fly out of a drink[5], a key to lock the door[6] and the 'treasure' box people would keep in their homes[7].

From all these examples, and many more that could be taken from the Gospel text, it is clear that Jesus took his words and images from people's day-to-day reality. He did this, not as a ploy, as an educational gimmick, to adapt himself to the 'lowly standard of his audience'. Rather, he employed familiar images for exactly the reason expressed much later by Freire: that people can only truly learn from within their own experience. Jesus' words and images were 'generative'. Taking them from people's own lives Jesus broadened their horizon, so that they could discover the *new* reality that should come about.

It also implies that in our own day and age Christians will have to find new generative words and images that correspond to the world we live in. Jesus' original words will always retain their validity; but they do not exclude, rather they demand, new formulations in terms relevant today. We have already looked

---

1. Matthew 24,41.

2. Matthew 9,16.

3. Matthew 9,17.

4. Matthew 23,23.

5. Matthew 23,24.

6. Matthew 23,13; see also 16,19.

7. Matthew 6,19-20; 13,52.

at this, from another angle, in the previous chapter. Jesus has set us free by starting the process of speaking 'generative' words.

In its marvellous document, *The Church in the Modern World*, Vatican II provides a good example of how the Church continues what Jesus had begun. The document picks up many generative words from technology, the human sciences, the social order, economics, the world's religious and political forces. These are called 'the signs of the times', recalling Jesus' rebuke to the scribes: 'You can predict the weather by looking at the sky. Why can't you discern the signs of the times?'[1] The document states:

> 'To continue Jesus' task the Church has always had the duty of reading the signs of the times and of interpreting them in the light of the Gospel. In language intelligible to every generation she can respond to the ever recurring questions which people ask about this present life and the life to come . . . .'[2]

Critical Reflection

Any teaching worthy of the name should stimulate critical thinking according to Paolo Freire. Good teaching is a process of dialogue in which teacher and student both explore part of reality and discover new truths. In the words of Freire: 'To speak a true word is to transform the world . . . . but no one

1. Matthew 16,3.

2. A.FLANNERY, *Vatican Council II*, Dublin 1975, p.905.

can say a true word *for* another.'[1] The teacher encourages the student to think for himself or herself. Is this the way Jesus taught?

Again, the answer is YES. Jesus did not attempt to pass on a body of knowledge people had passively to accept. Jesus wanted people's eyes to be opened. He wanted them *to see for themselves*. He complained about lack of response when he said in the words of Isaiah:

> 'This people listens and listens,
>   but does not understand.
> They look and look, but do not see.
> For their minds are dull.
> They have stopped their ears
>   and closed their eyes . . . .'[2]

The story of the man born blind speaks for itself.[3] Jesus cures the man of his blindness, but not without the man's own cooperation. First the blind man has to make his own way from the Temple area to the pool of Siloam. Jesus does not send an apostle to take him there by hand. After his cure, people do not want to accept his story. Then the man has to defend Jesus' action against the objections of the Pharisees who claim no one may practice medicine on the sabbath. Even his parents desert him saying: 'He is old enough. Let him speak for himself!'

But the blind beggar who was surely uneducated, gains confidence and begins to think critically. 'The man who opened my eyes is a prophet', he says. A little later: 'This is amazing! He

---

1. P.FREIRE, *Pedagogy of the Oppressed*, pp.75 - 82.

2. Matthew 13,14-15; compare Isaiah 6,9-10.

3. John 9,1-41.

has opened his eyes and you people don't know where he comes from! We know that God doesn't listen to sinners . . . . If this man were not from God, he could not do a thing.'[1] Eventually the man meets Jesus again and accepts him as his saviour. At the end of the episode Jesus concludes: 'I have come into this world so that those who are blind may see, and those who see may be blind.'[2] Conversion is a process of opening one's eyes and one's heart.

We should also note the paradox: 'the blind see, those who see are blind'. *Paradoxes* force us to think because they seem to express conflicting ideas. Jesus loved to present his message in such paradoxes.

> **'Who comes first shall be last, who comes last shall be first.'[3]**
> **'He who wants to be the first, should be the last of all.'[4]**
> **'He who is not for me is against me.'[5]**
> **'Whoever is not against us is for us.'[6]**
> **'Happy are you who hunger now,**
>   **you will be satisfied . . . ..**
> **Woe to you who are filled now,**

---

1. John 9,17 and 9,30-33.

2. John 9,39.

3. Matthew 19,30; 20,16.

4. Mark 9,35.

5. Matthew 12,30.

6. Mark 9,40.

you will go hungry!'[1]
'If the light in you is darkness,
  how dark it will be!'[2]
'Let the dead bury their dead!'[3]

Such paradoxes force people to think. Who are 'the first' or 'the last'? How are we 'for' or 'against' Jesus? What 'hunger' or 'darkness' is Jesus talking about? Who are 'the dead' that bury their dead? and so on. We discover that things are often not what they seem to be.

Questions open people's minds. The scribes were used to raising and discussing questions. More than once they bombarded Jesus with questions:

'Why do you eat with sinners and tax collectors?'[4]
'Why do your disciples eat corn on the sabbath?'[5]
'Why do you not wash your hands before the meal?'[6]
'On what authority dare you act like this?'[7]

Jesus in turn would ask questions of his own.

'I too will ask you a question. Tell me: did John's baptism come from heaven or from below?'[8]

---

1. Luke 6,21 and 6,24.

2. Matthew 6,23.

3. Matthew 8,22.

4. Luke 5,30.

5. Luke 6,2.

6. Luke 11,38.

7. Matthew 21,23.

8. Matthew 21,25.

'Have you not read what David did when he and his
followers were hungry . . . ?'[1]

'Which one of you will not pull his son out of a well
on a sabbath day, if the boy falls into it?'[2]

'Show me a denarius. Whose image and name are
on it?'[3]

'What is your opinion about the Messiah? Whose
son is he?'[4]

In fact, according to Luke's Gospel Jesus had already begun
to ask questions of the scribes during his visit to the Temple as a
twelve-years old boy. 'He sat among the teachers in the Temple,
listening to them and asking them many questions . . . .'[5]

Was an omniscient Jesus playing a game with the scribes?
No, Jesus 'grew in wisdom'[6] by sharing the searchings of
learned people. As with every mature person, the habit of listening and raising questions must have remained with Jesus
throughout his life. Although on many occasions he would teach
with authority and act with prophetic determination, on other
occasions he knew the doubts of the seeker.

'Father, what shall I say? Shall I say: 'Save me from

---

1. Luke 6,3.

2. Luke 14,5.

3. Luke 20,24.

4. Matthew 22,41-46.

5. Luke 2,46.

6. Luke 2,52.

this hour?"[1]
'God, my God, why have you forsaken me?'[2]

Jesus' desire to make his audience think also transpires from his frequent use of *parables*. A parable is a form of teaching closely related to the riddle. While a riddle could be devised with the simple idea of entertaining people,[3] the parable had a teaching purpose. Also, unlike the riddle, the parable is open-ended. Its meaning is not covered by one single application. It invites people to chew on what is intended, to discover layer upon layer of meaning.[4]

To ensure that the parables would make people think, Jesus did not, as a rule, explain them at once. Sometimes he would give an explanation to his apostles.[5] Even then his explanation was not given to 'close' the meaning; it was a pointer in the general direction.

What would people make of this enigmatic story?

> An unclean spirit who had left a man, roamed through the desert and could not find a place to stay in.
> 'Well, I'll go back to the home I left', it thought.

---

1. John 12,27. Questions are central to John's Gospel. In this Gospel alone we find 161 of them. For a discussion of their importance, see J.WIJNGAARDS, *The Gospel of John and his Letters*, Wilmington 1986, pp. 35 - 46.

2. Matthew 27,46.

3. Samson presented such a riddle to the Philistines; see Judges 14,12-18.

4. The meaning of Jesus' parables will be explored more fully in the WALKING ON WATER book, *The Signs of the Kingdom*.

5. Compare Matthew 13,4-9 and 13,18-23.

**When it returned, it found the place vacant, swept and
tidy. So it went off again and collected seven other
spirits more evil than itself.**

All went in and set up house in that place.[1]

What unclean spirit was Jesus talking about? What warning did
he give?

Or consider the parable of the children on the market place.
People would wonder what Jesus meant by it. In the story, some
of the children complained: 'We played the pipes for you and
you wouldn't dance; we sang funeral hymns and you wouldn't
mourn'.[2] Who were the players and who the sulkers?

The Gospel tells us that teaching parables was a matter of
principle for Jesus.

All this Jesus told the crowds in parables.

Without parables he told them nothing.

This was to fulfil the prophecy:

'I will open my mouth to you in parables.

I will expound things hidden from the beginning.'

Matthew 13,34-35[3]

By reflecting on his parables people would gradually discover
the new 'kingdom of God' Jesus was proclaiming to them.

Challenging oppressive structures

A third skill which Paolo Freire requires good teachers to
pass is the ability to discern 'problems'. He also calls this
'uncovering limit situations': situations that limit people's free-

---

1. Matthew 12,43 - 45.

2. Matthew 11,16 - 17.

3. See also Psalm 78,2.

dom and so need to be overcome. The teacher has to start the process of challenging the forces that oppose freedom. Did this apply to Jesus?

Jesus did not see himself first and foremost as a social reformer. And, as we saw in the previous chapter, there were many injustices in his time which, within his own limitations, he could not address. But he *did* start the process of challenging forces that curtail people's freedom. Jesus often acted and spoke as a prophet who denounced what was wrong.[1] And of special interest are those instances where Jesus pointed out that language was being used as a form of manipulation.

People often use language to deceive and manipulate. Words then become a tool of oppression. People say things in a clever way to gain an advantage over others. Jesus disapproved of this use of language.

Jesus abhorred the way in which political rulers could impose their authority and demand public titles of honour as well. 'The kings of the pagans lord it over their people. Those who exercise power are given the title 'benefactor'.'[2] Jesus does not want the apostles to act in the same way. That is why he wants them to avoid such honorary titles as 'Teacher', 'Father' and 'Leader'.[3]

Jesus told the parable of the unjust steward who cleverly changed his master's accounts to make friends among the

---

1. Examples are: Jesus' driving the merchants from the Temple square (Mark 11,15-17); his cursing the fig tree (Matthew 21,18-19); his rebuke to Peter (Mark 8,33).

2. Luke 22,25.

3. Matthew 23,7-11.

farmers who owed him money.[1] Jesus decried the way in which the scribes and Pharisees laid heavy burdens upon people's shoulders by their supercilious demands.[2]

Jesus rejected the use of language by persuasive salesmen, clever politicians or hypocritical preachers.

This is what Jesus taught about human words:
> **'Judge a tree by its fruits.**
> **No good tree produces rotten fruit,**
> **nor does a bad tree produce healthy fruit.**
> **You cannot harvest figs from a thorn bush**
> **or grapes from a bramble.**
> **A good person produces good from the store of goodness**
> **in his heart.**
> **A bad man draws what is bad from his store of evil.**
> **For a person' words flow out of what fills his heart.'[3]**

---

1. Luke 16,5-8. Jesus says we can learn from the man's astuteness, even though he was wrong committing a fraud. The man who finds the treasure in the field, covers it up and buys the field, presumably does not tell the owner about the treasure. He, too, cheats (Matthew 13,44). What we can learn from such people is, for example, their single-minded commitment.

2. Matthew 23,1-36.

3. Luke 6,43-45.

Freedom of faith and conscience

Christians are people whom Jesus expects to think for themselves. Fundamentalists who cast Jesus in the role of an authoritarian and paternalistic preacher, have invented a similar role
for Church leaders. But this was not Jesus' idea, nor is it the
teaching of the Church. Yes, the Church *has* authority to
present doctrine and lay down moral guidelines, but these are
not to be imposed from above. They are given to believers who
have the duty and the freedom to assimilate them in their own
personal act of faith and their own individual conscience. No
one can believe for us or make moral decisions for us.

Here are some statements of Vatican II in its *Declaration on
Religious Freedom*:

'Each human person has a right to religious freedom. This
freedom means that all people should be immune from
coercion by individuals, social groups or any human
power, so that in religious matters no one is to be forced
to act in a manner contrary to one's own beliefs . . . .'

'Truth is to be sought after in a manner appropriate to
the dignity of the human person and his social nature,
that is: the enquiry is to be free, carried on with the aid of
teaching or instruction, communication and dialogue. In
the course of these, people explain to each other the
truth they have discovered, or think they have discovered,
in order to assist one another in the quest for truth. And,
as the truth is discovered, it is by a personal assent that
people are to adhere to it . . . .'

'In the formation of their own consciences, Christian
believers should carefully attend to the sacred and certain
doctrines of the Church. The Church is, by Christ's will,

136

the teacher of the Truth. It is her duty to express, and authoritatively, to teach, that Truth which is Christ; and also to declare and confirm by her authority principles of the moral order . . . .'[1]

The important thing is to realise that Christ's authority as a teacher and the freedom of the believer do not exclude each other. In fact, Christ's teaching, and in our own time the Church's teaching, truly set us free by giving us the guidance by which we ourselves can of our own accord commit ourselves to faith and to a Christian life.

---

1. *Declaration*, no 2, 3 and 14. A.FLANNERY, *Vatican Council II*, Dublin 1975, pp.799-812; see also W.M.ABBOTT, *The Documents of Vatican II*, New York 1966, pp.675-696.

QUESTIONS FOR PERSONAL STUDY

1. Christ wanted us to accept his message as free, mature and responsible people. How then could he make this demand?

> **'Unless you change and become like children,**
> **you shall not enter the kingdom of heaven.'**
>
> (Matthew 18,3-4)

Does a child not leave thought and decision to his parents?

2. The Church has authoritative teaching power in doctrinal and moral matters. Christ said to the apostles:

> **'Whatever you bind on earth shall be bound in**
> **heaven.**
> **Whatever you loosen on earth shall be loosened in**
> **heaven.'**   (Matthew 18,18)

Does this not restrict the freedom of Christian believers?

3. Vatican II says:

> **It is to be hoped that more lay people will receive**
> **adequate theological formation and that some**
> **among them will dedicate themselves professionally**
> **to these studies and contribute to their progress.**
> **For the proper exercise of this function, let it be**
> **recognised that *all* the faithful, both clerical and**
> **lay, possess a lawful freedom of inquiry, thought**
> **and expression.**
> **Let this expression be both humble and courageous**
> **in whatever branch of study they have specialised.'**
>
> *The Church in the Modern World*, no 62.

Is theology the preserve of priests and religious? What makes us theologians?

MONEY AND POWER

The Gospel tells us that Herod Antipas, king of Galilee, arrested John the Baptist and had him executed. The story is well known in all its gruesome details: Herodias' grudge against John; Herod's birthday party which was attended by 'the chief government officials, army officers and leading citizens of Galilee'; Salome's dance; the girl's demand for John's head to be brought on a dish; and John's execution itself.[1] The news shocked Jesus. He withdrew for some time to a lonely place, probably on the other side of the lake.[2]

Jesus was shocked, but he was not surprised. He knew the political realities of the time. He was aware of the power structures that kept his people in a tight hold. As is always the case, power ultimately rested on economic control. In this chapter we will look at Jesus' world from this perspective. It will help us grasp the distinctively *religious* vision which Jesus proposed.

Romans and Herodians

At the time of Christ Palestine was part of the Roman Empire. This meant that the Roman Emperor who resided in Rome, was the highest political authority. For all practical purposes Palestine was a colony, a province ruled by Rome

---

1. Mark 6,17-29; Matthew 14,3-12.

2. Matthew 14,13.

through local leaders or through Roman administrators. When Jesus began his ministry the Emperor was Tiberius and the Roman Governor of Judaea was Pontius Pilate. Galilee was not ruled directly by the Governor, but by a local king, Herod Antipas.[1]

Who were these Romans?

They came from Rome, a city in Italy that produced good soldiers and capable organisers. Through centuries of military successes, Rome began to flourish with ever greater wealth and prosperity. To keep up this prosperity required further conquests. In the course of time this led to the establishment of a formidable empire that engulfed all the countries around the Mediterranean Sea, from Spain in the west to Syria in the east, from Britain in the north to Egypt in the south.

The Roman empire maintained its control through military domination, political rule and efficient taxation.

The Roman armies excelled in discipline and the imaginative use of the latest technology. In Italy itself Roman citizens were drafted into the legions; in countries outside Italy, foreign mercenaries were enrolled. But these too were drilled in all the skills the Romans mastered so well: hand-to-hand combat, assault and defence in formation, building fortifications and siege works, subduing unruly crowds and marching long distances at short notice.

Roman soldiers were well armed for battle (see illustration). A short tunic covered with brass plates protected the body. A helmet was worn and a buckler. The lance, the javelin and a stubby, two-edged sword functioned as their main weapons.

---

1. Luke 3,1.

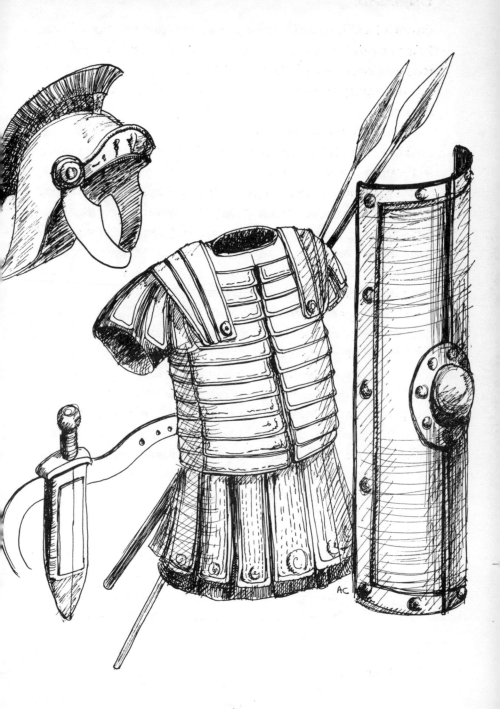

To keep the troops mobile and well supplied called for good lines of communication. The Romans developed a network of paved roads that connected all corners of the empire to Rome. Sea routes were supervised. A fleet was maintained, new ports opened.

The Romans were too intelligent to impose one rigorous, uniform rule on all subjected nations. They encouraged local government, as long as the indigenous rulers ensured the steady flow to Rome of taxes and favourable trade. The status of the Roman 'man-on-the-spot' varied from being merely a military observer to being totally in charge. The Roman strong man could be a proconsul, a legate, a procurator or a prefect.[1]

*The Romans had a standard arrangement for their army camps (see the illustration on the right). A fortified camp (**castra**) was occupied by a **cohort** of six hundred men.*

> *a. defensive ditch*
> *b. rampart wall*
> *c. twin gates with d. a guard room*
> *e. military headquarters*
> *f. house of the **tribune** in command*
> *g. granary*
> *h. barracks for legionaries*
> *i. officers' quarters for **centurions***
> *j. workshops and stores*
> *k. hospital and clinic*
> *l. baths*
> *m. latrines*

---

1. It was thought for a long time that Pontius Pilate was 'procurator'. In a recently found inscription he is given the title of 'praefectus', one notch lower on the hierarchical scale.

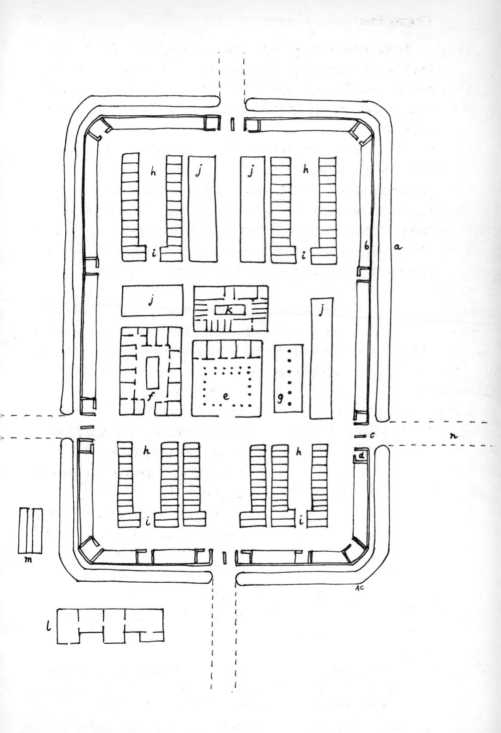

The Romans recognised Palestine as a particularly difficult country because of the Jews' opposition to foreigners on religious grounds. The Emperors tried to cooperate with a number of competing political factions. Eventually they settled on the Herodian family. Their support of Herod the Great brought a measure of success. He managed the local politics well and remained loyal to Rome. Herod's sons proved more of a problem. Gradually the Romans took more and more direct control over the province. This would provoke the Jewish rebellion of 67 AD and the Roman-Jewish war (68 - 70 AD) that resulted in annexation, destruction and exile.

For the ordinary people in Galilee it mattered little who ruled at the top. They felt the daily pressure of heavy tax burdens and of the trade monopolies the Romans had imposed. The common man and woman saw the world as a pyramid of oppressive powers with themselves at the bottom of the heap. Slaves and servants were subject to their masters. These were responsible to land owners, local governors and petty officials. These in turn were under supervision of Herod's court in Tiberias. Herod Antipas himself was under constant control of Roman colonial power.

If in the land you see the poor oppressed and right and justice trampled under foot, do not be surprised. For every official has another higher than himself on top of him, and above these are others higher still . . . . 'The produce of the earth is for all', they will tell you. 'Farming supports the king.'[1]

---

1. Kohelet 5,7-8; freely translated.

GOVERNMENT OF PALESTINE

63 BC   Pompey conquers Palestine for Rome.

39 BC   Herod the Great begins to rule Palestine
with the support of Emperor Augustus.

4 AD   *Jesus is born in Bethlehem.*
Herod the Great dies.
Augustus divides Palestine among Herod's sons.

Judea and Samaria	**Galilee and Perea**
Archelaus king of	**Herod Antipas** king
Judea and Samaria.	of Galilee and Perea.

7 AD   Augustus deposes Archelaus.
From now on Roman Governors
rule Judea and Samaria.

26 AD **Pontius Pilate** appointed
Governor of Judea and Samaria.

27 AD   *Jesus begins his public
ministry in Galilee.*

30 AD   *Jesus is put to death by
Pontius Pilate in Jerusalem.*

36 AD   Pontius Pilate deposed as
Governor.

39 AD   Herod Antipas dies.

Large estates

It was the Greeks who introduced more efficient ways of farming to Galilee, as they had done in other parts of the Middle East. Under the Ptolemaid kings of Egypt, and later the Seleucid kings of Antioch, these improvements were applied mainly to the 'crown lands', estates which were immediate royal property and over which the king appointed his own managers.

To the traditional crops of wheat, barley, olives and vines, new crops were added of greater economic value like balsam in the plain of Gennesareth, flowers for honey, pomegranates and mushrooms. Varieties of high yield were selected and bred. Wells were dug for systematic watering and canals for irrigation.[1] Farming operations like ploughing, sowing, weeding, pruning and harvesting were undertaken by seasonal workers under supervision of permanent staff. Researchers tells us that a revolution was taking place, a change over from an economy of 'mutuality' to an economy of 'agro-business'.[2]

The traditional farmer produced a limited range of goods: wool, grapes and wheat, perhaps. These were partly used for the family's own needs, partly exchanged for other goods, like

---

1. One example is the royal estate of Beth Anath. A certain Glaukias reports (in a letter dated 257 BC) that new strains of vine have been introduced to the estate and that another well has been dug. The estate, we are told, has 80,000 vines in culture. M.HENGEL, 'Das Gleichnis von den Weingärtner im Lichte der Zenonpapyri', *Zeitschrift der neutestamentlichen Wissenschaft* 59 (1968) pp. 1 - 39.

2. S.FREYNE, *Galilee from Alexander the Great to Hadrian*, Wilmington 1980, pp. 170 -176; see also *Galilee, Jesus and the Gospels*, Dublin 1988, pp. 155 - 175.

oil and wine, which were also needed by the family.[1] In agro-business goods were turned into money. Traditional farmers might also sell some produce for cash, but only to facilitate the exchange process; they looked on farming as way of living, not as an industry.

Business farms tended to specialise, or, just the opposite diversify, for purely commercial reasons. Vast expanses of land were devoted to one crop. The harvest would be stored in huge barns. Export markets were sought where the produce could be sold for the maximum profit, sometimes overseas so that daughter industries grew up: the fabrication of *amphoras*[2] for oil and wine, the construction of ships to transport the merchandise. The ultimate aim was monetary gain, part of which the owner would plough back into his business to improve performance.

The Holy Land, including Galilee, could have benefited a lot from such an agricultural revolution. Unfortunately, the development got side-tracked in a number of ways. First of all, the improvements hardly touched the small landowners. Farmers in the villages who managed to hang on to their own plot of land, continued to farm in the old traditional ways. Secondly, a small group of elite families began to concentrate wealth. They acquired the previous crown lands and any other estate they could lay their hands on. In Galilee, for instance, Herod Antipas possessed such estates, as did a number of his officials. Some

---

1. Jesus lifts the old principle of mutuality to a higher level when he says: 'Do to others as you would like them to do to you; that is the meaning of the Law and the Prophets.' Matthew 7,12.

2. These were earthenware vats that could hold about twenty litres. Two handles for lifting were fixed on the side. The top could be sealed with a tight-fitting cap. The bottom was pointed for easy storage on top of (and between) other amphoras.

rich land owners lived in Sephphoris, Tiberias and Jerusalem.[1]

These landlords were often reluctant to spend capital on agricultural change; they simply wanted to make as much profit as possible. Capital was spent on amassing more land. Small farmers frequently could not meet the debts they had incurred by a combination of drought, high taxes, disease in the crop or other disasters. The rich land owner would step in, buy the farmer out and make him work for himself as a tenant.

The figure of **the landlord** can be recognised in a number of Gospel passages.

* When Jesus spoke of 'those dressed in fine clothes who live in palaces',[2] people knew he meant their absentee landlords who owned splendid residences in Hellenistic cities.
* A prominent citizen declines the king's invitation to attend the wedding of a prince because 'I've just bought a field'.[3]
* One landlord feels he should build more spacious granaries because of a plentiful harvest. 'I've made it', he says to himself. 'I'm alright for years to come. From now on I can eat and drink and enjoy life.'[4]

1. D.J.HERZ, 'Grossgrundbesitz in Palästina im Zeitalter Jesu', *Palästinajahrbuch* 24 (1928) pp 98 - 113.

2. Matthew 11,8.

3. Luke 14,18.

4. Luke 12,16-21.

Jesus also refers more than once to the post of **the manager** appointed by the landlord. These managers supervised the tenants, collected their master's share and kept the accounts. Probably they received a percentage of the income as payment.

* A manager of crown lands owes the king 10,000 *talents* (34 kilograms of gold each), probably in revenue he has failed to collect. The king cancels this debt - an amount too large for ordinary people even to imagine! The manager then meets one of his tenants who owes him 100 *drachmas* (silver coins of 4 1/2 grams each), but he does not show the poor man the same generosity the king had shown him.[1]

* A rich man who goes to a far country, entrusts ten, five and one talent to three servants. The first two do good business with their master's capital. They are rewarded by being put in charge of 'ten villages' and 'five villages'. This undoubtedly means that they are now made managers of large estates which virtually encompassed whole villages.[2]

* A crooked manager who is going to be sacked by the land owner, makes friends of his tenants by reducing their debts on the credit notes.[3]

Jesus knew, and deplored, the abuses and injustices that accompanied the interaction of landlord, manager and tenants on large estates. But he did not condemn the system as such. In

-----

1. Matthew 18,23-34.

2. Luke 19,11-27.

3. Luke 16,1-9.

fact, he saw many human angles in it from which we can learn to create a better world. We too are managers - in the Father's kingdom! From secular managers we can learn planning and foresight, creative enterprise and a sense of responsibility.

> **'The children of this world are more astute in handling their affairs than the children of light'.[1]**

> **'To every one who achieves something, more will be given.'[2]**

The parables teach us to keep our priorities right, to remember God's values and to treat others as God would treat us.

Did Jesus address these parables to landlords and managers?

Yes and no.

Among his audience there were some who belonged to this class. One of the women who followed Jesus was 'Joanna, whose husband Chuza held a post at Herod's court'.[3] Then there was the rich young man who wanted to be Jesus' disciple and for whom the family estate proved an insurmountable obstacle.[4]

But the majority of his audience were ordinary people. They knew landlords by repute and estate managers from day-to-day contact.

---

1. Luke 16,8.

2. Luke 19,26.

3. Luke 8,1.

4. Matthew 19,16-24.

The ordinary people

We have already met the common folk of Galilee, when we discussed Capernaum and Nazareth. Now we must assess them from an economic point of view.

In the countryside there were still quite a number of farmers who owned their own plot of land.[1] The father Jesus speaks of in his parable of the prodigal son, was going to leave the family property to his two sons.[2] Another man owned a small vineyard and depended on his sons to work in it.[3] Though independent, these subsistence farmers were not likely to become millionaires.

Taxes weighed heavily on profits. The Romans levied a poll tax for each member of the family and took a quarter of the produce as land tax, to be delivered every second year. The religious authorities in Jerusalem exacted a tithe and Temple tax. Enterprising farmers who wanted to sell their produce outside their region, faced crippling custom duties at each border. A sales tax on market goods was operated in cities and towns. What remained was scanty indeed.[4]

Farmers had no insurance against drought, mildew, locusts or other natural disasters. Their stores were often plundered by gangs of rebels or highway robbers. Passing soldiers were billet-

1. M.GIL, 'Land Ownership in Palestine under Roman Rule', *Revue Internationale des Droits de l'Antiquité* 17 (1970) pp. 11 - 53.

2. Luke 15,11-31.

3. Matthew 21,28-32.

4. F.C.GRANT, *The Economic Background of the Gospels*, Oxford 1923; E.SCHUERER, *A History of the Jewish People in the time of Jesus*, New York 1961, pp 189 - 192.

ed in the villages. None of these misfortunes excused farmers from paying their taxes. Loans might tide them over for a while; often they ended in total ruin as interest could be as high as 25 per cent. Jesus refers to the hard reality of a householder being forced to sell himself, his family and his property to settle a debt.[1] At other times he mentions debtors being thrown into prison and subjected to torture until the last penny had been paid up.[2]

Many small farmers escaped such a drastic fate by agreeing to sell their freehold and become tenants instead.[3] It hardly improved their condition. Now they had to hand over even more of their crop as the owner's share, while having lost ownership of the land.[4]

Against this background we can understand the parable of the tenants of the vineyard. They were hostile to the owner and to the various middlemen the owner sent to collect his share. The vineyard in this parable is Israel, and God the owner.[5]

---

1. Matthew 18,25. Some records seem to indicate that there was a thriving slave trade from Palestine to Egypt.

2. Matthew 5,25-26; see also 18,30 and 18,34.

3. It has been claimed that the tenants were actually slaves or bondsmen, but that was apparently not the case. Agricultural slavery, as practised in Italy, was not common in the Middle East. P.BRIANT, 'Laoi et Esclaves Ruraux', in *Actes du Colloque 1972 sur l'esclavage*, Paris 1974, pp 93 - 133; esp. pp 96 - 106.

4. Some tenants paid a share of the crop, others had to pay a fixed amount irrespective of the prevailing conditions. S.APPLEBAUM, 'Economic life in Palestine', *Compendium Rerum Judaicarum ad Novum Testamentum*, ed.M.STERN and S.SAFRAI, vol.2, pp. 631 - 700.

5. Isaiah 5,1-7.

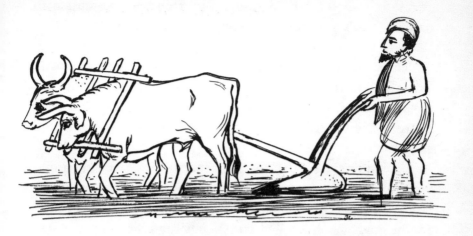

'No one who puts his hand on the plough and looks back is fit for the kingdom of God' (Luke 9,62).

Farmers used rather primitive ploughs. They were not so much preoccupied with keeping the furrow straight as with keeping the plough down. Since the soil was bumpy and dry, a farmer needed to press the plough down all the time to ensure that the blade would cut the soil deeply enough. It is this single-minded commitment a disciple should have.

'Put on my yoke and learn from me . . . .
For my yoke is easy, my burden light' (Matthew 11,29-30)

Jesus uses two parallel images here: the yoke put on an ox who pulls the plough and a burden put on a donkey for transportation.

The images of the Gospel speak with more force the more we can vividly picture daily life in the Holy Land. A book I can recommend is: R.GOWER, <u>Manners and Customs of Bible Times</u>, Amersham-on-the-Hill 1987.

Jesus compares the leaders of Israel to hostile tenants who oppose God's prophets and, when they meet Jesus, say: 'He is the heir. Let us kill him!'[1]

The small craftsmen in the towns and villages were so closely associated to the farmers that they did not really constitute a separate class. Here we may reckon carpenters(=builders), potters, the village scribes, fishermen, local merchants and shopkeepers.[2]

Lowest on the scale of social prosperity lived the rural proletariat, the people who neither owned nor leased land and exercised no skilled profession. These were casual workers taken on for the day,[3] shepherds,[4] hired servants[5] and slaves[6].

These then were the ordinary people of Galilee, a motley crowd of mixed origin, varied status and divergent occupation, yet roughly sharing the same conditions of life. For all ultimately lived off the land.[7]

The problem was: did they really *share* what they had in common? Or did they fight each other in heartless competition?

---

1. Matthew 21,33-46.

2. The Hellenistic world had a middle class with a more distinct social niche. A.N.SHERWIN-WHITE, *Roman Society and Roman Law in the New Testament*, Oxford 1963, pp. 139 - 140. See also W.MEEKS, *The First Urban Christians*, London 1984.

3. Matthew 20,1-16.

4. John 10,12-13.

5. Mark 1,20.

6. Luke 17,7-10.

7. A.OPPENHEIMER, *The Am Ha-Aretz. A Study in the Social History of the Jewish People in the Hellenistic-Roman Period*, Leiden 1977.

The rule of mammon

Jesus, we can be sure, was appalled by the way the powerful exploited the poor. But we misunderstand him if we think that his main concern was the overthrow of Galilee's rulers. He upheld the authority of the Roman emperor saying: 'Give to the emperor what belongs to the emperor'.[1] He did not condemn the system of agro-business as such. He did not preach the kind of social revolution advocated by political reformers.

As usual, Jesus' vision of reform was far more fundamental, and therefore ultimately far more subversive to systems of exploitation. Jesus saw that one root cause of the social disorder lay in allowing *money* to dominate relationships. Land, capital and profit dictated what people said and did to each other.

And this basic submission to greed and self-interest affected the ordinary people as much as the very rich. The poor might have an initial advantage: 'Happy are you who are poor, the kingdom of God belongs to you!'[2]; but only if their true treasure is with God.[3] For among the ordinary people too there were those who were better off but did not help their neighbours; or those who tried to climb the economic ladder over the backs of others.

> *   Zaccheus was not a wealthy landlord. He was probably a farmer's son who wanted to advance in life and who chose to become a custom official because of its lucrative prospects. He made

---

1. Matthew 22,21.

2. Luke 6,20.

3. Matthew 6,19-21.

profits on duties squeezed out of other people like himself.[1]

*   Stealing was only too common. People kept their best clothes and jewellery in a locked chest, but even then they were not safe.[2]

*   A woman has saved ten drachmas (= ten days' wages) for some special purpose. When she finds one is missing, the suspicion of a theft may have entered her mind. Was it her husband? One of her children? Or, perhaps, she has dropped the coin. Being silvery in appearance it is not easily spotted on the clay floor. Imagine her relief when she does find it![3]

*   Anxious farmers stayed awake at night fearing thieves might plunder their granary.[4]

*   Those appointed to oversee a large household often treated their fellow servants badly. They beat them up, withheld their wages or failed to give them proper food and drink.[5]

*   A spiteful villager might sow weeds among the wheat crop of a neighbouring farm.[6]

---

1. J.R.DONAHUE, 'Tax Collectors and Sinners. An Attempt at Identification', *Catholic Biblical Quarterly* 33 (1971) pp 39 - 61.

2. Matthew 6,20; Luke 12,33.

3. Luke 15,8 - 10.

4. Matthew 24,43.

5. Luke 16,1-6.

6. Matthew 13,24-30.

* Travellers might find a robbed and wounded fellow traveller on a lonely desert road and leave him to die.[1]

People's hearts had grown hard. They thought no longer as God does - who prizes and loves each human person. They had begun to worship money rather than God.

'No one can serve two masters at once.
He will either hate the first and love the second,
or treat the first with respect and the second
with contempt.
You cannot serve both God and money.'[2]

What the world needed was a new scale of values.

1. Luke 10,30-37.

2. Matthew 6.24.

QUESTIONS FOR PERSONAL STUDY

1. What are your comments on this incident:

   A man in the crowd said to Jesus, 'Master, tell my brother to give me my share of our inheritance'.

   'My friend', Jesus replied. 'Who appointed me judge or arbitrator in your case?'

   Then he stated: 'Be on your guard against every kind of greed . . . .'

   Luke 12,13 - 15

   Had you expected Jesus' warning?

2. After recounting the parable of the crooked manager Jesus makes this remark:

   'Whoever is faithful in small matters will be faithful in large ones.

   Whoever is dishonest in small matters will be dishonest in large ones.'

   Luke 16,10

   What does Jesus mean?

3. Vatican II enunciates this basic economic principle:

   In the sphere of economics and social life, the dignity and total vocation of the human person must be respected and promoted, along with the welfare of society as a whole.

   For human beings are the source, the centre and the purpose of all socio-economic life.

   The Church in the Modern World, no 63

   Can you see some implications of this principle for our present-day world?

Space for your own notes

THE KINGDOM OF GOD

During many long years Jesus prepared for his mission in the comparative solitude of Nazareth. He absorbed all aspects of the reality that enveloped his people, the people of Galilee. He was one of them. He thought like them. He spoke their language. He felt in his own bones what they feared and what they were hoping for.

But Jesus also found in himself something different. He discovered that God, his Father, was pulling him in a certain direction. He began to see things the way his Father saw them. He began to understand the ancient promises the Father had made to generations of his ancestors. He felt a new power surging up in himself, a vision of what the Father wanted, an anticipation of things to come that could turn the whole world upside down. And the moment came when he knew that he himself had been chosen to be the person through whom the Father was going to speak and act.

This is when Jesus began to announce *the kingdom of heaven*.

'Kingdom of heaven' is an image of the new reality his Father was going to bring about. Dozens of classical studies have been written on what exactly Jesus meant with this image.[1]

---

1. To mention just a few major publications (in English editions): J.WEISS, *Jesus' Proclamation of the Kingdom of God* (1900); A.SCHWEITZER, *The Mystery of the Kingdom of God* (1925); E.F.SCOTT, *The Kingdom and the Messiah* (1911) and *The Kingdom of God and the New Testament* (1932);

Scholars continue to debate a number of questions concerning the image, but on its general outline there is wide agreement.[1]

To begin with, in 'kingdom of heaven', *heaven* stands for *God*. This can be seen from the many instances in which the Gospels mention 'kingdom of *God*' as an obvious equivalent.[2] 'The kingdom of the Father' also occurs.[3] To avoid mentioning God by name, the Jews often used 'heaven' when they meant 'God'. They would say: 'I have sinned against heaven'[4] and 'We don't know whether this is from heaven or from human beings'.[5] Think also of our own expression: 'Heaven forbid!' kingdom of heaven therefore means: God's kingdom.

The word *kingdom* needs clarification too. When we speak about a kingdom, we usually think of <u>a country</u> that is ruled by a king. We can then say that someone travelled the

---

...Continued...

W.MANSON, *Christ's View of the Kingdom of God* (1918); C.H.DODD, *The Parables of the Kingdom* (1935) and *The Kingdom of God and History* (1938). A 446-page classic that is still available and that has been updated is: G.R.BEASLEY-MURRAY, *Jesus and the Kingdom of God*, Grand Rapids 1986.

1. R.SCHNACKENBURG, *God's Rule and Kingdom*, New York 1963; G.E.LADD, *Jesus and the Kingdom*, New York 1964; B.CHILTON (Ed.), *The Kingdom of God*, Philadelphia 1984; N.PERRIN, *The Kingdom of God in the Teaching of Jesus*, London 1963, and *Jesus and the Language of the Kingdom*, Philadelphia 1976.

2. Four times in Matthew; fifteen times in Mark; twenty-seven times in Luke.

3. Matthew 6,10; 6,33; 13,43; 26,29.

4. Luke 15,18.

5. Matthew 21,25-26.

length and breadth of the kingdom, or that there was a war between two kingdoms, and so on. This is not the first and most important meaning of *malkûth*, 'kingdom', for the Jews. *Malkûth* meant someone's '<u>being</u> king', what we may render by *kingship* in English. God's kingship means that God is king. This was what the prophets kept telling Israel. God had punished his people for their sins, but in the future he would be their king once more.

> 'The Lord of Hosts will be king
> on Mount Zion, in Jerusalem.'
> > *Isaiah 24,23*
>
> 'How lovely on the mountains are the feet of the herald
> who proclaims good news . . . .
> who tells Zion: 'Your God is king!' '
> > *Isaiah 52,7*
>
> 'Shout for joy, daughter of Zion . . . . ,
> The Lord has repealed your sentence,
> he has swept away your enemies.
> The Lord is in your midst as king, O Israel.
> You have no more evil to fear.'
> > *Zephaniah 3,14-15*

When Jesus announced that the kingdom of heaven had come, he was in fact saying: 'God's kingship has come'. 'God is king once more.' 'God rules over us again.'

> **Jesus began to preach: 'Repent, for the kingdom of heaven has come near!'**
> > *Matthew 4,17*
>
> **'If it is by the finger of God that I cast out demons, then the kingdom of God has come upon you!'**
> > *Luke 11,20*

'Go and proclaim that the kingdom of heaven has come near.'

Matthew 10,7

The kingdom of God is not coming with external signs. People will not say: 'See, it is here!' or 'See, it is there!' For the kingdom of God is within you.'

Luke 17,20-21

Scholars are agreed that Jesus preached God's kingdom within the *apocalyptic* expectations of his time. Jesus' contemporaries expected that a revelation (*apocalypsis*) of God's kingship was imminent. In the Assumption of Moses, an apocalyptic writing of the time, we read:

'Then God's kingdom shall appear throughout his creation.

Then Satan shall be no more . . . .

For the Heavenly One shall arise from his royal throne.'[1]

And the Essenes in Qumran looked forward to God's rule.

'You, O God, radiant in the splendour of your kingdom,

you are in our midst as a perpetual help . . . .'

'To Israel's God shall be the kingdom.

Among his people he will display his power.'[2]

In fact, in the *Kaddish* prayer which Jesus' contemporaries recited every day, people asked God to establish the kingdom in their life time.[3]

---

1. *Assumption of Moses*, no 10. R.CHARLES (ed.), London 1897.

2. *The War Scroll*, IQM 12,7 and 6,6.

3. See page 89 above.

'The Lord is king!'
'Play the lyre
for our God!'
    Psalm 147,7

Read the enthronement
psalms: no 93, 95, 96,
97, 98, 99, 149, 150.

Jesus responded to these apocalyptic expectations of his people. But the interpretation he gave of what God's rule means exceeded their thoughts and hopes.

God's Rule

There are very few kings or queens left in the world and where they still exist they are, to a great extent, no more than figure-heads of national unity. For most of us it is easy to forget how central the position of a king was in ancient society.

In tribal societies like Israel, the community resembled a large family and the king was an overall father; possessing, as father, absolute power and ultimate responsibility. Under a good king the whole family of society flourished; under a bad king everyone suffered hardship.[1] The king was at once lawgiver, supreme judge and army chief. In Israel, in spite of influences from neighbouring nations, the tribal image of a king who is close at hand and paternalistic remained predominant.[2]

This is also how Jesus understood God as being king. For him God was above all 'the Father'. In harmony with the traditional ideas about kingship and fatherhood, this implied both God's absolute authority and his loving concern. Jesus fills these attributes with a new depth of insight.

The Father exercises complete control. He makes the ultimate decisions in Jesus' life. The Father calls Jesus to his

---

1. Read, for example, 1 Samuel 8,10-18.

2. C.J.GADD, *Ideas of Divine Rule in the Ancient East*, London 1948; M.NOTH, 'Gott, König und Volk im Alten Testament', *Zeitschrift fr Theologie und Kirche* 47 (1950) pp. 188 - 223.

mission.[1] The Father reveals Jesus' messiahship to Peter.[2] The Father decides who will sit at Jesus' right hand or left hand.[3] Only the Father knows when the last judgment will take place; he has not told the Son.[4] Jesus will act as judge on the Last Day, but he will only do so on behalf of the Father.[5] The verdict will depend on Jesus accusing or defending a person before his Father.[6] It is the Father who will give the final pardon.[7] Everything in this world depends on the Father's will.[8] Jesus himself always tries to do the will of his Father.[9]

But God also possesses the tender love of a good father. Jesus called God *Abbâ*, the everyday Aramaic word for 'Daddy'.[10] In this Jesus was absolutely unique. None of his contemporaries dared to employ such a familiar term. It was a distinctive feature of Jesus' own praying and preaching.[11]

---

1. Matthew 3,16-17; 17,5.

2. Matthew 16,17.

3. Matthew 20,23.

4. Mark 13,32.

5. Matthew 25,34.

6. Matthew 10,32-33.

7. Matthew 18,35.

8. Matthew 10,29; 18,14.

9. Matthew 26,39-42.

10. Mark 14,36; compare Galatians 4,6; Romans 8,15.

11. J.JEREMIAS, *The Central Message of the New Testament*, London 1965, pp. 9 - 30; *Abba. Studien zur neutestamentlichen Theologie und Zeitgeschichte*, Gottingen 1966, pp. 15 - 67.

The <u>anemone coronaria</u>, with its red and blue flowers, is one of the common 'flowers of the grass' that cover Galilean meadows after the rains in spring.

Jesus was impressed by the care 'his heavenly Father' bestowed on these simple creatures. Had his Father not given them a dress more splendid than the ornate robes of King Solomon?

If God treats the grass like this, how much more will he look after us . . . . (Matthew 6,28 - 30).

Jesus filled the image of God as father and king with people's everyday experiences of parental love and care. God is a forgiving father who looks forward to his wandering son coming back home.[1] God tolerates his children even if they are selfish and ungrateful.[2] Like a good father, God will not give us a snake if we ask for an egg.[3] We need not worry about food and dress or other small matters; as a good father God knows we need these.[4] God loves us and cares about us as a loving father would.

God, our loving Father, is king. He is in total command. He is taking responsibility. He cares. He wants our good. He invites us to repent and come back to him. All these ideas are implied in the image of the kingdom of heaven. I propose to combine all these ideas in the expression: **God's rule**. God's rule has begun. This world is now becoming once more God's world. God is our Father who rules us with his loving concern.

There are many implications in Jesus' notion of God's rule. Some of them will be discussed more fully in other books of our WALKING ON WATER series. In Jesus God has revealed himself as Father, Son and Spirit.[5] Jesus has set us free from our sins and from all religious powers that keep us estranged from God.[6]Through God's rule we who believe,

1. Luke 15,11-32.

2. Luke 6,35-36.

3. Luke 11,11-13.

4. Luke 12,30.

5. *God is Close*, WALKING ON WATER, no 6.

6. *Religion of the Heart*, WALKING ON WATER, no 4.

become one family in the Church.[1] The kingdom of God works on us through the sacraments and the liturgy.[2] Since in this book we concentrate on Jesus' *people*, I will restrict myself here mainly to the consequences of God's rule for human relationships. If God is our father, then we are all brothers and sisters.[3]

Relationships

For God's rule to become a reality in our world we have to accept God's priorities. We saw in the previous chapter how money had begun to dominate people's lives. That was wrong. Jesus put it simply as an incompatibility: 'You cannot serve God *and* money'.[4] God's first priority is the good of people.

That this is really God's priority follows from the prophecy of Isaiah which Jesus read to his family in Nazareth:

> **'The Spirit of the Lord is upon me.**
> **He has chosen me to bring good news to the poor.**
> **He commissions me to proclaim freedom for captives**
> **and sight for the blind,**
> **to set the oppressed free**
> **and announce the Lord's year of grace.'**
> *Luke 4,17*[5]

---

1. *Gospel and Community*, WALKING ON WATER, no 1.

2. *The Signs of the Kingdom*, WALKING ON WATER, no 5.

3. Matthew 12,50.

4. Matthew 6,24.

5. Isaiah 61,1-2. See also above, pp. 68 - 69.

God's rule is Good News because it sets people free. The image in the prophecy derives from an ancient custom in Israel, namely that every seven years, at the beginning of the *sabbath* year, all debts were cancelled and slaves were set free.

> 'At the end of every seven years you must grant a release. And these are the terms of the release: Everyone who has lent money to a fellow-Israelite must cancel the debt.'
>
> 'If a fellow-Israelite, man or woman, is sold to you as a slave, you are to release him after six years. When the *sabbath* year comes, you must let him go free.'[1]

The holy year, the Lord's sabbath year, was really good news to the poor. God's year of grace which led up to a complete renewal of the Covenant,[2] also relieved the physical hardships of many people. The year of grace Isaiah speaks of includes both the spiritual and material uplift God will provide to his people. In Jesus' time the cancelling of debts was no longer practised literally; but Jesus saw the important *social and spiritual* implications of the old custom. If God renews his relationship to us, then we too should renew our relationships to each other.

One obvious application lies in forgiveness. If God forgives us (as he does in his new kingship), we too must forgive each other. This was so important to Jesus that he incorporated it into his model prayer, the Our Father.

> **'Forgive us our debts,**
> **as we also forgive those who are in debt to us . . . .'**

---

1. Deuteronomy 15,1 - 18; here verses 2 and 12.

2. Deuteronomy 31,9-13.

> **Yes, if you forgive others their faults,**
> **your heavenly Father will forgive you yours.**
> **But if you do not forgive others,**
> **your Father will not forgive your failings either.'**
>
> *Matthew 6,12-15*

Jesus worked this out even more fully in the parable of the unforgiving manager. The king had cancelled the man's debts of 10,000 talents, but the manager insisted on his own tenant paying 100 denarii. In his anger the king condemns the manager to be sent to prison till his whole debt was paid. Jesus concludes with these words:

> **'My heavenly Father will deal with you in exactly the**
> **same way, if you do not each forgive your brother from**
> **your heart.'**
>
> *Matthew 18,35*

Jesus is saying clearly: your relationship to God cannot be in order, unless you have resolved your relationship to other people. Our making peace with people is more important than anything else, even more important than offering sacrifice.

> **'If you are bringing your offering to the altar and there**
> **you remember that your brother (or sister) has some**
> **thing against you,**
> **leave your offering there before the altar,**
> **and first go to make peace with your brother (or sis-**
> **ter).**
> **Only then come back and present your offering.'**
>
> *Matthew 5,23 - 24*

In other words: God can wait. The question of being reconciled to your brother or sister cannot wait. God will not make peace with you, unless you have made peace with the people around you.

Neighbourly love

Charity towards others is not a law which God imposes from above. Charity and love are the stuff God's rule, God's kingdom, is made of. Where love between people is lacking God cannot be present as king. That is why Jesus praises the scribe who has understood that the love of God and love of the neighbour are together the greatest commandment. 'You are not far from the kingdom of God', Jesus told him.[1]

In fact, the two forms of love belong so closely together that when we appear before God at the last judgment, we may expect to be examined on how we related to God. We might think God will talk about what we did for him in prayer or worship. Instead, he will put these questions to us:

'Did you give me food when I was hungry?

Did you welcome me into your home when I was a stranger?

Did you share your clothes with me when I had none?

Did you look after me when I was sick?

Did you visit me when I was in prison?'

And when we are then confused and do not know what to answer, he will say: **'Whatever you have done to the least of my people, you have done to me.'**[2]

Could there be a stronger way of Jesus telling us that for God people are *the* priority? In God's world people always come first.

---

1. Mark 12,28-34.

2. Matthew 25,31 - 46.

Images of the kingdom of God

When Jesus tried to explain what was happening with the coming of God's kingdom, he often resorted to telling the stories which we call parables.

He would begin the parable with a characteristic turn of phrase: the kingdom of heaven can be compared to this or that.

'The kingdom of heaven is
 like a man who had grown good seed in his
  field . . . .[1]
 like a mustard seed which a man planted . . .[2]
 like yeast which a woman mixed in flour . . . .[3]
 like a treasure hidden in a field which someone
  found . . . .[4]
 like a merchant who was looking for beautiful
  pearls . . . .[5]
 like a net thrown out upon the sea . . . .[6]
 like a king who wanted to settle accounts with
  his servants . . . .[7]

---

1. Matthew 13,24.

2. Matthew 13,31.

3. Matthew 13,33.

4. Matthew 13,44.

5. Matthew 13,45.

6. Matthew 13,47.

7. Matthew 18,23.

> like a householder who went out early in the
> morning to hire workers . . . .[1]
> like a king who arranged the feast for his
> son's wedding . . . .[2]
> like ten girls who were going to meet the
> bridegroom . . . .[3]

Jesus compares the kingdom of heaven to various *stories*, not to things. That is why in modern translations the opening of the parables is rendered differently. 'The kingdom of heaven is like this. A man had sown good seed in his field, etc.' Jesus sees some comparison between the whole situation described in the parable and what happens in the world when God is king.

We have stated before that Jesus used parables deliberately to make us think.[4] A parable is 'a metaphor or simile drawn from nature or common life, arresting the hearer by its vividness or strangeness, and leaving the mind in sufficient doubt about its precise application to tease it into active thought'.[5] By making us think about God's rule through parables, Jesus indicated that it was something to be discovered, something that has to 'grow' on us.

The last thing Jesus wanted was for us to have a static idea of God's Kingdom. For there is a vast difference between fixed, closed ideas and open-ended images. The same word can stand for both.

---

1. Matthew 20,1.

2. Matthew 22,2.

3. Matthew 25,1.

4. See above, pp. 131 - 132.

5. C.H.DODD, *Parables of the Kingdom*, London 1935, p. 7.

Take the term *workshop*. In the context of a furniture business, it has a very precise meaning. The 'workshop' stands here for the physical place where joiners and carpenters shape the wood. 'Phone later. John is in the workshop' leaves no shade of doubt. The meaning is closed. But when I say: 'Let's call together some experts for a workshop on this problem', I am using the word as a metaphor. I know roughly what it means, but it remains open-ended. It could turn out to be no more than an informal consultation; it could equally well result in a professional seminar.

Or think of *marriage*. The word is precisely defined by law. Civil magistrates can determine without much hesitation who is married and who not. If two people *are* married, they receive well circumscribed rights and duties. Because of the legal dimensions as little as possible is left to imagination. Everything is laid down to the letter. This is marriage as a fixed concept. But when a trade agreement between the United States and Russia is described as 'a marriage of East and West' it has become an image. We know what is meant, but new horizons are implied: the love that binds the two partners, future offspring, permanent commitments, and so on. The term is open-ended.

The word *kingdom of heaven* is clearly open-ended for Jesus.[1] Its hard-core meaning is clear: God is setting his people free. The consequence is that we should also set each other free. But Jesus did not determine the details for all time to

1. Scholars speak of the Kingdom of God as steno-symbol (= a closed idea) or as a tensive symbol (= an open-ended image). For an explanation of these terms, see P.WHEELWRIGHT, *Metaphor and Reality*, Bloomington 1962, p. 92; N.PERRIN, *Jesus and the Language of the Kingdom*, Philadelphia 1976, pp. 29 - 32; 197 - 199.

come. He wanted us to be inspired by the *image* so that we could continue to give creative, new interpretations to God's action and our own response.

This openness to the future and to unexpected growth is a feature of God's kingship itself. Who would have thought that a tiny black grain so small that one can hardly see it, can grow into a tree big enough for birds to nest in its branches?[1] Jesus dreams in this image not only of his band of followers growing into a world-wide community of believers, but also of all the unforeseen ramifications God's revolution could bring about in the world. Similarly, the small pinch of yeast that leavens the enormous mass of dough,[2] expresses the extent his new values could penetrate society. They are beautiful images which he left us to work with in our own way. Through them he invites us to continue his initiative with the same breadth of vision.

Changing our world

When Jesus looked around him in Galilee, he saw plenty of things that would need to change if people were to respond to God and live in his kind of world. He overwhelms us with examples.

> * Like the Good Samaritan we must help any person we meet on our way and who is in real need.[3]

---

1. Matthew 13,31-32.

2. Matthew 13,33.

3. Luke 10,29 - 37.

* Learning from the story of the Pharisee and the tax collector, we should not look down on others.[1]
* We should not be like the elder brother of the Prodigal Son who did not welcome him home.[2]
* We should take great care to save those in trouble, treating them as if they were a lost sheep which we seek till we find it.[3]
* We should be merciful, and be peacemakers.[4]
* We should not dominate others as political leaders often do, but render service in humility.[5]
* When we invite people to dinner, we should not ask our relatives and friends, but the poor, the crippled, the lame and the blind; those who cannot repay us.[6]

These are just examples of what new relationships under God's kingship could look like in Galilee.

In modern society Jesus' vision of a new world will affect relationships on many levels. Without claiming to be exhaustive in my listing, I would like to hint at some of the implications.

1. Luke 18,9 - 14.

2. Luke 15,25 - 32.

3. Matthew 18,10 - 14.

4. Matthew 5,7.9.

5. Matthew 18,1-4; 20,24 - 28.

6. Luke 14,12 - 14.

There is, to begin with, the international order. Organisations like the United Nations, the World Health Organisation, the UNESCO for culture and UNICEF for children, deserve our full support. Third World countries should be given a fair chance. We should not tolerate discrimination against any person because of their origin or colour of skin.

Other people have a right to clean and healthy living. We have a responsibility to use the world's resources sparingly, sharing what we have with others as fairly as possible. We may not pollute or destroy the living space of others because of our own short-sighted gains.

In society all persons should have equal rights. There should be an equitable division of property. The rights of all sectors of society should be protected. Provision should be made to support those in special need, like the unemployed, the homeless, orphans, immigrant workers and one-parent families. The kingdom of God has many implications for our political choices.[1]

In our dealings with the people we meet, we should maintain truly human relationships, resisting the walls technology is erecting within our world. We should give people the time they need and allow them to have their feelings and express them. At all times people should have the first priority in our scale of values.

---

1. CH.ELLIOTT, *Praying the Kingdom. Towards a Political Spirituality*, London 1985.

None of such implications are spelled out by Jesus in modern terms. Yet they flow naturally from his vision. We could summarise all of them as flowing from a radical demand of *mutuality*. Mutuality was the basis of tribal justice, of family care and village economy.[1] Already the Old Testament contained the advice: 'Do to no one what you do not want done to you'.[2] In the new dispensation of the kingdom of heaven this guideline has been turned into a positive principle and has been extended to all human relationships.

> **'Treat other people exactly**
> **as you would like them to treat you.**
> **That is the meaning of the Law and the Prophets.'**[3]

But was mutuality the only demand made by God's kingship? Certainly not. Mutuality was only the first stage, the minimum, the start of the revolution that can transform human relationships. There was more to Jesus' vision; as we shall see in the next chapter.

---

1. See our discussion of it on pages 146 - 147 above.

2. Tobit 4,15.

3. Matthew 7,12. The expression 'the Law and the Prophets' refers to the whole Old Testament; to the totality of God's revelation at the time.

QUESTIONS FOR PERSONAL STUDY

1. When Jesus teaches us to pray,
    'Father, hallowed be thy name,
    thy kingdom come . . . .'   *Luke 11,2,*
what exactly is it that he wants us to pray for?
And, will the prayer mean the same for every person?

2. What do you make of this saying of Jesus?
    'Since John the Baptist came, up to this present time, the
    kingdom of heaven has been subjected to violence.
    And the violent are taking it by storm.'
                    Matthew 11,12

3. Please, read this excerpt from Vatican II and comment on its
meaning.
    'Although we must carefully distinguish secular progress
    from the growth of Christ's kingdom, such progress is of
    vital concern to the kingdom of God in as much as it
    contributes to the better ordering of human society.
    First we must obey the Lord and his Spirit by nurturing
    on earth the values of human dignity, brotherhood and
    freedom, as well as all the good fruits of human enter-
    prise. Then, afterwards, we will find them again, now free
    of the stain of sin, enlightened and transfigured. This will
    be when Christ will hand over to the Father a universal
    and eternal kingdom: a kingdom of truth and life, of
    holiness and grace, of justice, love and peace.

    On this earth that kingdom is already present as a mys-
    tery. When the Lord returns, it will be brought to full
    perfection.'
                    The Church in the Modern World no 39.

THE OVERFLOWING MEASURE

When we discussed Nazareth I mentioned that, though it such a small hamlet, it lay close to a mountain from which one had marvellous views.[1] I am sure that Jesus, the village handyman, often sat on that mountain top and gazed at the wider world. There he must have prayed to God the Creator, his Father and his King. There he must have reflected on the wider implications of his Father's kingship.

The Gospels record more than one incident that happened on top of a mountain. Some of these may have theological significance for the evangelists, but there can be little doubt about their preserving at the same time a historical trait of Jesus' personality. He liked tops of mountains. That is where he preferred to pray. That is where the Father communicated to him the width and breadth of his vision.

* **He went up the mountain to pray by himself.[2]**
* **Jesus went to the mountain to pray and he spent the whole night there praying to God.[3]**
* **Taking Peter, John and James with him, Jesus went up the mountain to pray. And while he was praying his face was transformed and his clothing became brilliant**

---

1. See page 67 above.

2. Matthew 14,23.

3. Luke 6,12.

> **as lightning . . . . A cloud came and overshadowed them, and a voice from the cloud said: 'This is my Son, whom I have chosen. Listen to him.'[1]**

Sometimes Jesus also taught on the top of a hill. It gave Matthew the idea to put many of Jesus' special teachings together in one sermon which he makes Jesus deliver on top of a mountain: the sermon on the mount.[2] Matthew has his own theological reason for doing this. As the old covenant was proclaimed on Mount Sinai, so Jesus proclaims the Father's new covenant from another Sinai. The ten commandments of Sinai are updated with the eight beatitudes of Jesus.[3] But there was another good reason for putting this teaching of Jesus on a mountain. For here Matthew has brought together many sayings of Jesus that speak of 'the extra', of 'what is more', of how relationships in the *kingdom* should transcend and excel.

Wholeness in the kingdom

Whatever failings the Pharisees and scribes might have, everyone knew they were anxious to fulfil the Law to the dot. They strove with all their might to attain 'justice', perfect sanctity, as demanded by God. What then to make of this extraordinary statement?

> **'I tell you, if your sanctity does not excel that of the scribes and Pharisees, you shall not enter the Kingdom of Heaven.'[4]**

---

1. Luke 9,28-36.

2. Matthew 5,1; 8,1.

3. Compare Exodus 19,2 - 20,21 and Matthew 5,1-12.

4. Matthew 5,20.

As if to reply to the question of what this extra sanctity means, Matthew gives us a number of examples.

* One of the ten commandments says: 'You shall not kill'. The scribes had worked out in detail who should be brought to trial on the charge of murder. But Jesus said we should not even be angry with someone else or insult the other with offensive names. Rather, we should take the initiative of making peace.[1]

* Another of the commandments forbade adultery. Jesus pointed out that chastity is not only violated by deeds. Chastity begins in our mind and in our attitude.[2]

* Old Testament Law allowed divorce and the scribes debated what constituted a sufficient ground for divorce. Jesus upheld the principle of the indissolubility of marriage.[3]

* The scribes argued about the obligations resulting from vows and oaths. Jesus maintained that there was something wrong in us having to swear an oath at all.[4]

* The scribes stuck to the rule of equal revenge. *An eye for an eye and a tooth for a tooth.* Jesus declared that we must outdo others in tolerance and forbearance. We should turn the other cheek, give our cloak

---

1. Matthew 5,21 - 26.

2. Matthew 5,27 - 30.

3. Matthew 5,31 - 32; 19,3 - 9. See also the discussion on pages 105 - 108 above.

4. Matthew 5,33 - 37.

as well if someone takes our tunic, go an extra mile if we are forced to carry a pack.[1]

In all these examples we notice that the extra consists in doing more than is required by the Law because we care about what is at stake. We do not observe the minimum. We give more than is strictly required. We obey the Father, not according to the letter, but according to the spirit of what he desires. We go beyond mutuality because we want to give generously.

God himself always gives generously. Sometimes we have to push him, to insist - like the friend who needs a loaf of bread in the middle of the night (see illustration).[2] Eventually God will give because creation means giving.

The hallmark of the *kingdom* is generosity. Paul records Jesus' principle that there is more happiness in giving than in receiving.[3] But, remarkably enough, if we *give* generously, generously we will receive.

'Give to others, and God will give to you.

A full measure,

> **pressed down,**

> **shaken together and running over,**

he will pour into your lap.

The measure you use for others is the measure God will use for you.'[4]

---

1. Matthew 5,38 - 42.

2. Luke 11,5 - 8.

3. Acts 20,35.

4. Luke 6,38. Literally: 'Give and it will be given to you'. This is a so-called *theophoric* passive, a passive form that implies God. The Jews would use this passive form to avoid mentioning God by name.

Working on a higher principle

To grasp Jesus' way of thinking we should, perhaps, look at its concrete application to human relationships. Here too, Jesus tells us, we should go beyond a *quid pro quo*, beyond mutuality. We should forgive rather than retaliate. We should give more than we receive.

Jesus' ideal of charity has frequently been badly misinterpreted, both inside and outside the Christian Churches. The American philosopher Ayn Rand has attacked it in her many publications. According to her, Christian charity degrades people because it treats others with patronising condescension. Rather than speak of love and generosity, we should reaffirm every person's dignity. The only real love is self-love. When we do something for someone else, we do it because we receive an equivalent gift in return. That is the only sound basis for human relationships.[1]

Rand has a point. There have been Christians, and perhaps there are still, who call 'charity' what is no more than their duty; or who by so-called 'charity' disguise their lack of doing justice; or who 'dispense charity' in a patronising and condescending manner. But this was not Jesus' idea.

> *Leaving ninety-nine sheep to look for one stray one is the logic of the kingdom. God is happier about one sinner who converts than about ninety-nine respectable people who do not need conversion, Jesus said (see Luke 15,4-7)!*

---

1. A.RAND, 'The Virtue of Selfishness' in *For the New Intellectual*, New York 1961. She expresses the same ideas in her novel, *The Fountainhead*, New York 1962.

As we saw in the previous chapter, relationships in the *kingdom* are first and foremost based on mutuality. If mutual rights and obligations are not granted, the 'extra' gift makes no sense. And mutual justice implies full respect for the other person and acknowledgement of what he or she gives to us.

It is also clear that there are situations when we will have to act on strict principles of mutual justice. The penal system, even in a Christian society, will need to incorporate punitive measures to deter criminals. Civil laws will uphold people's right to restitution for damages. In certain circumstances we will have to stand up for our rights and claim what is ours. Jesus too realised this. In spite of his principle of 'turning the other cheek', he challenged the soldier who slapped him on the face in his hearing before Annas.[1] And, not withstanding his aversion from oaths, he responded in court when he was put on oath by the high priest.[2]

Where Rand goes wrong is in not seeing that a higher principle can be at work which does not contradict mutuality but supplements and surpasses it. Suppose that some enmity has arisen between two persons. Both have reason to complain about the other's behaviour. Well, if they keep on paying each other in kind, there will never be an end to their fight. In order to get out of their impasse, they must rise *above* mutuality and make peace.

This is the higher principle Jesus advocated. He believed so strongly in it that he repeated it in different forms. The world will never realise true peace and harmony unless

---

1. John 18,22 - 23.

2. Matthew 26,62 - 64.

people can adopt an attitude that transcends their immediate, narrow horizons.

The following text is an absolute classic:

> **'Love your enemies.**
> **Do good to those who hate you.**
> **Bless those who curse you**
> **and pray for those who treat you badly . . . .**
> **If you love those who love you,**
> **what blessing is in it?**
> **Even sinners love those who love them.**
> **And if you do good only to those**
> **who do good to you,**
> **what blessing is in that?**
> **Even sinners do that much.**
> **And if you lend only to those**
> **from whom you hope they can pay you back,**
> **what blessing is in that?**
> **Even sinners lend to sinners,**
> **to get back the same amount.**
> **No,**
> **love your enemies and do good to them;**
> **lend and expect nothing in return.**
> **You will then have a great reward**
> **for you will prove to be children of the Most**
> **High God.**
> **He himself is kind to the ungrateful and the**
> **wicked.'**
>
> *Luke 6,27 - 35*

According to Jesus, there is no 'blessing' in just giving *quid pro quo*. If we truly are children of God who live under his kingship, we will transcend a short-term view of things and decide to be patient, kind, forgiving, never mind how people respond. We will be loving on principle; not because others are patient, kind and forgiving to us, but because our goodness will eventually, in the long term, win the upper hand. There is blessing and reward in such an attitude, not only in the sense of us finding favour with God, but in our improving the overall situation itself. This is a higher logic. It is God's logic, Jesus saw. He does not abandon his kindness even if people oppose him. God provides rain and sunshine to good and bad alike.[1]

This unshakable inner goodness of God derives from God's wholeness. The word Jesus used was *thamîm*. In translations it is often rendered by 'perfect' (via the Greek). But *thamîm* means 'whole'.[2] Jesus saw that we too should have this inner wholeness in us, as God has it in himself.

> **'If you greet only your relatives, what extra is it**
> **you are doing?**
> **Don't the pagans do the same?**
> **No, you must be whole**
> **as your Father in heaven is whole.'[3]**

'What extra is it you are doing?'

'This sentence is the key to this whole chapter of Matthew. It is the answer to the question: How does the disciple differ from a pagan? What makes him a Christian? This key sentence sums up all the rest: the truly Christian element is what is extraordinary, extra, more than normal, different from the usual, the not so obvious. This is the justice that transcends

---

1. Matthew 5,45.

2. In the Old Testament it is applied to Noah, Abraham and the people of Israel; see Genesis 6,9; 17,1; Deuteronomy 18,13.

3. Matthew 5,47 - 48.

the justice of the Pharisees, that excels, that goes beyond, that towers over it . . . . That is why a Christian can never totally conform to the world. He has to hold on to *the extra*'.[1]

Meeting violence head on

The higher principle Jesus advocated has its repercussions in politics too. This also is an area where Christians have often neglected their duty. As all other citizens, Christians are responsible for the welfare of their society. They should take an active part in politics to ensure that justice is done to all.

What happens if a particular society is governed by an oppressive regime?

Can Christians resort to arms to defend their rights and bring about a political revolution?

If the principles of self defence and the defence of one's property are accepted, why are poor people who are deprived of their rights not allowed to rise up in self defence?

In previous centuries many Christians were confused about the correct response. Some were mesmerised by scriptural texts that state that political authority comes from God.[2] Some maintained that the division between social classes was willed by God and should not be disturbed. Others again held that oppression and suffering in this world would be offset by rewards in the hereafter. There was a real need for a complete rejection of such totally inadequate and crippling views and the

1. D.BONHOEFFER, *Navolging*, Amsterdam 1964, p.135. See also: F.BOERWINKEL, *Meer dan het gewone*, Baarn 1977, esp. pp.58 - 70.

2. John 19,11; Romans 13,1 - 5.

formulation of a more realistic Christian response. This has now been offered especially in the liberation theology worked out by the Churches of Latin America.[1]

If we may summarise liberation theology in a nutshell, it derives from three major insights, each leading to a commitment:[2]

1. The true meaning of biblical salvation includes liberation in every aspect. Christian theology should be committed to full human liberation.

2. Complete biblical salvation has to be achieved in the actual, historical world. Christian theology is bound to view everything from a concrete, functional point of view.

3. Theological language and social structures are politically and mentally interdependent. Christian theology is committed to a praxis which is both biblically inspired and realistic.

---

1. Some classical works available in English are: G.GUTIER-REZ, *A Theology of Liberation*, New York 1976; H.ASSMANN, *Theology for a Nomad Church*, New York 1976; J.L.SEGUN-DO, *Theology for Artisans of a New Humanity*, New York 1973, and *The Liberation of Theology*, New York 1976; J.M.BONINO, *Doing Theology in a Revolutionary Situation*, Philadelphia 1975; E.DUSSEL, *History and the Theology of Liberation*, New York 1976. The statements of the Latin American Bishops' Conferences gathered in Medellín in 1968 and Puebla in 1979 made the thrust of a programme of Christian liberation the official policy of the Church for the continent; *The Church in the Present-Day Transformation of Latin America in the Light of the Council*, Bogotá 1968.

2. J.L.SEGUNDO, 'What is common in all theology of liberation?', in *Theology for the Americas*, New York 1976, pp. 280 - 283.

From a Scriptural point of view, the new perspective made scholars look again at the Gospels with new eyes. What was the social condition of the society in which Jesus lived? In what ways did Jesus himself engage in the process of social liberation? What can we learn from him about the dialectical tension found in present-day liberating praxis: the tension between a utopian dream and concrete action within a historical, conflictive process? It led to new studies on Jesus and Christology.[1]

The Brazilian Leonardo Boff tells us that for Jesus Christ 'the Liberator', the kingdom of God possesses two meanings, one negative, the other positive. The negative meaning, he says, implies rejection of this world as it is now. The *kingdom* is against poverty, hunger, hatred, the exploitation of fellow human beings, legalism, pharisaism, false religion, sin, and death. In its positive meaning, the *kingdom* promotes love, justice, healing, the fullness of life and the total transformation of this world according to the plan of God.

Establishing the *kingdom* exacts a price.

'The concrete steps of historical liberation are always conflictive and burdensome. All true liberation rests upon a covenant of blood and death. All the prophets, both of yesterday and today, know this; the prophet cannot be worried about his own neck. No prophet ever died in his bed. It is the same with Jesus, the Liberator par excellence.'[2]

---

1. J.SOBRINO, *Christology at the Crossroads*, New York 1978; J.L.SEGUNDO, *The Historical Jesus of the Synoptics*, New York 1985.

2. L.BOFF, *Jesus Christ Liberator. A Critical Christology for our Time*, New York 1978.

In practical terms, a programme of liberation entails a decisive option for the poor, the promotion of conscientisation at all levels,[1] adopting critical techniques of economic analysis, using all available democratic means to expose injustice and defend the poor.

As Boff pointed out, people who opt for the poor often find themselves arrayed against powerful oppressors. Jesus himself experienced this. He came up against the brute force of the Roman army which, for political reasons, sided with Jesus' religious accusers. Not counting the persecution of innumerable lay leaders, during the last ten years alone more than 400 priests and religious were killed in Latin American countries by right-wing para-military groups.

The crucial question remains: can the institutional violence of repressive political systems be overthrown with counter-violence?

Camilo Torres, born in Bogotà in 1929, was ordained a priest, studied sociology at Louvain in Belgium and returned to Colombia in 1958. He dedicated himself heart and soul to the liberation of the poor. In June 1965 he reached the conclusion that justice for the poor could only be obtained through violence. Laicised by the Church, he joined a guerrilla force, the Army of National Liberation. One year later his detachment ambushed a military patrol and Camilo was killed.

Camilo justified violence on the principle that love should be effective. The old-style 'charity' - alms, a few tuition-free schools, a few housing projects - had not succeeded in feeding the hungry majority, clothing the naked, or teaching the unschooled masses. Since power was held by the ruling *élite*,

---

1. See page 117 above.

who refused to share it equitably, such power *must* be taken from the privileged minorities and given to the poor majorities. Thus revolution was unavoidable.

> 'Revolution is the way to obtain a government that will feed the hungry, clothe the naked and teach the unschooled.
>
> Revolution will produce a government that will carry out works of charity, of love for one's neighbours - not for only a few but for the majority of our neighbours.
>
> This is why revolution is not only permissible, but *obligatory* for those Christians who see it as the only effective and far-reaching way to make the love of all people a reality.'[1]

I believe we have to respect the testimony of Camilo Torres and many others who have followed his path. There *are* historical situations that demand from Christians that they take up arms and meet violence with counter-violence. This may well involve joining a guerrilla force and promoting an armed revolution. The actual conditions and one's own informed Christian conscience will justify and prompt this response. Nothing I will say in subsequent paragraphs should obscure this clear statement.

However, the preferred option for Christians should be a peaceful one.

---

1. C.TORRES, *Frente Unido*, 2 September 1965; *Revolutionary Priest. The Complete Writings of Camilo Torres*, ed. J.GERASSI, Penguin 1971, p. 374.

Active non-violence

In the context of Jesus' vision of God's kingship it should be recognised that Jesus advocated non-violence as the ordinary Christian response. It is interesting to note that this also seems to be the almost universal stand of those involved in the Latin-American Christian struggle for liberation. Helder Camara, Archbishop of Recife in Brazil, put it in words.

> 'I respect those who feel obliged in conscience to opt for violence - not the all too easy violence of armchair guerrillas - but those who have proved their sincerity by the sacrifice of their lives . . . .
> My personal vocation is that of a pilgrim of peace. Personally I would prefer a thousand times to be killed than to kill.'[1]

Jesus advocated the use of non-violence as an example of the higher logic of the *kingdom*. Again, we can reflect on this with the help of a practical example.

The Catholic community of Northern Ireland bears deep scars inflicted by centuries of Protestant oppression. Some members of the community resort to acts of terrorism as a means of furthering what they believe is the solution: political unification of the North to the predominantly Catholic Republic of Ireland. Protestant para-military groups retaliate with counter acts of violence. Even without entering the claims and counter-claims made by either side, one can see that the way out is not *only* establishing complete justice. Love will have to

---

1. From a lecture given in Paris, 25 April 1968; S.CASSIDY, *Audacity to Believe*, London 1978, p. 317. Cassidy gives an excellent picture of the institutional violence in Chile of the 1970s. See also: A.MORELLI, *Libera a mi pueblo*, Buenos Aires 1971.

enter, to heal and to make both communities discover the true value of the other. A spiral of violence that has begun will not stop unless both parties forgive and forget.

A disturbing finding by sociologists is that in quite a few countries Christians justify violent means more easily than non-Christians. The cause of this astounding fact seems to lie in a distorted image of God.

In some forms of Christian spirituality, God is credited with a 'liking' for suffering. God the Father is seen as a hard God who insisted that his own Son suffer and die: he would not grant redemption without seeing blood. The same hardness is then translated into an inclination towards authoritarian solutions, towards militarism and the violent suppression of opponents.[1]

I have refuted this horrendous misunderstanding in other publications, trying to show that God is truly a God of love and that Jesus' sacrifice was not due to the Father's cruelty.[2] I have also written a novel about the same topic. It explores the extent to which misguided Christian spirituality can go.[3]

---

1. R.FRIEDLI, *Attitudes to Peace*, Address at the Inauguration of the RC Lectureship, Selly Oak College, Birmingham 1980.

2. J.WIJNGAARDS, 'Escape from the Cannibal God', *Inheriting the Master's Cloak*, Ave Maria Press, Notre Dame 1985, pp. 21 - 30; 'The Father is a God of Love', *The Gospel of John*, Michael Glazier, Wilmington 1986, pp. 145 - 155; 'The True Sacrifice', *The Tablet*, 25 March 1989, pp. 342 - 343.

3. J.WIJNGAARDS, *For the Sake of His People*, McCrimmons, Great Wakering 1990.

Jesus recommended the radical love that overcomes evil by good. As we have seen above, we should show love to our enemies and do good to those who hate us. In Jesus' time, violence was felt most by the heavy hand of the Roman occupation. Jesus too must have resented the injustices and hardships inflicted on his people. He must have endorsed the valid aspirations of those who wanted to restore Jewish independence.

But Jesus did not himself want to enter the scene as a political liberator. He refused to be made king by the people.[1] Also, he did not want the image of 'the kingdom of heaven' to be narrowly interpreted as a political reform. The prayer 'Thy kingdom come' does not mean: 'Thou wilt establish a new Israelite State', but: 'Thy will be done on earth as it is in heaven.'[2] Jesus knew that his option for the poor and his demands of radical justice would have political and social consequences. But he saw it as his own task to introduce the values of the *kingdom* from which these consequences were to flow.

Jesus was also non-violent on principle.
'I tell you: Do not oppose who does you evil.
If someone slaps you on the right cheek, present the other cheek too.
If someone takes you to court and demands your tunic, give him your coat as well.
And if anyone orders you to go one mile, go with him an extra mile.'[3]

1. John 6,15.

2. Matthew 6,9 - 10; see also page 91 above.

3. Matthew 5,39 - 42.

This last example may well refer to the practice by the occupying Roman soldiers of commandeering passers-by to carry their luggage.[1]

When Jesus entered Jerusalem shortly before his passion, he deliberately chose to enter the city seated on a donkey. He knew that the horse was the symbol of wealth, military force and political power (see the Roman officer in the illustration). He did not want his mission to be construed in such terms.

The greatest example of Jesus' non-violent approach is his own passion and death. Although he knew he was innocent, he forbade his disciples to defend him with the force of arms.[2] Jesus saw himself as the non-violent, suffering Servant of Yahweh who offered his life as a vicarious sacrifice for 'the many', that is: the whole of humanity.[3] In his own case the higher principle produced undreamed of results. The same kind of 'productivity' will result from the sacrifices of Jesus' followers.

> **'Amen, Amen, I tell you,**
> **unless a grain of wheat falls on the soil and dies,**
> **it remains only a single grain.**
> **But if it dies, it bears abundant fruit.'[4]**
> **'Deny self, take up the cross and walk in my steps . . .**
> **Anyone who loses life for the Gospel will save it.'[5]**

------

1. This is what happened to Simon of Cyrene; Mark 15,21.

2. Matthew 26,51 - 53.

3. This has been worked out well by J.JEREMIAS, *The Eucharistic Words of Jesus*, London 1966, esp. pp. 225 - 231; *New Testament Theology*, London 1971, pp. 276 - 299.

4. John 12,24.

5. Mark 8,34 - 35.

The limitless horizon

Throughout this book we have shown that Jesus loved his own people, the Galileans. His own immediate pastoral ministry was directed to them.[1] After his death and resurrection which took place in Jerusalem, Jesus returned to Galilee, as it were to put his seal on his own people and his own country.[2]

But the higher principles of the *kingdom* made Jesus transcend these narrow boundaries. Even during his ministry itself, he never excluded those who belonged to other nations.

* Jesus healed the slave of the Roman centurion stationed in Capernaum.[3]

* Jesus cured the daughter of the Canaanite woman in the region of Tyre and Sidon.[4]

* Jesus was tolerant towards the Samaritan village that refused him hospitality.[5]

* He healed a Samaritan leper and praised him for his gratitude.[6]

* He made a Samaritan the model of true neighbourly love.[7]

---

1. Matthew 10,5 - 6; 15,26.

2. See page 13 above.

3. Matthew 8,5 - 13; Luke 7,1 - 10.

4. Mark 7,24 - 30; Matthew 15,21 - 28.

5. Luke 9,51 - 56.

6. Luke 17,11 - 19.

7. Luke 10,29 - 37.

*   Jesus stayed and preached in the Samaritan village of Sychar.[1]

The Gospels record these incidents precisely because they were exceptions. Jesus could limit himself to his ministry among his own people because the message of *the kingdom* would be carried by his disciples to other nations throughout the world. To the man he cured in the Gerasene country Jesus said:

> **'Go home to your own people.**
> **Tell them all that the Lord in his mercy has done for you.'[2]**

It is Christ's injunction that is still with us today.

He calls on us go out 'to make disciples of all peoples'[3] and to be his witnesses to the ends of the earth.[4] But, wherever we are, he wants us to bring *the kingdom* to those we meet. Jesus wants us to give ourselves totally to our people or the people we have adopted as our own.

> **'Amen, Amen, I tell you,**
> **those who believe in me will do the same things I am doing.**
> **Yes, even greater things than I have done will they do, for I am going to the Father.'[5]**

---

1. John 4,1 - 42.

2. Mark 5,19.

3. Matthew 28,19.

4. Acts 1,8; see Luke 24,47 - 48.

5. John 14,12.

QUESTIONS FOR PERSONAL STUDY

1. Many people struggle to make ends meet. They cannot help worrying about how to stay alive. Are the values of *the kingdom* realistic?

> **'Don't be upset, worrying all the time about what to eat and what to drink.**
>
> **It is the pagans of this world who keep worrying about these things. Your Father knows that you need them.**
>
> **No, be concerned with his *kingdom*, and he will provide you with the other things.'**   *Luke 12,29 - 31*

2. In a world so full of injustice, how can we fail to notice and condemn what is wrong? But Jesus tells us (Matthew 7,1-2):

> **'Do not judge, and God will not judge you.**
>
> **For God will mete out the same judgment to you**
>
> **which you mete out to others.**
>
> **The norm you apply is the norm he will apply to you?'**

What higher principle is at stake here?

3. Reflect on the implications of this statement in Vatican II:

> **'The Lord also desires that lay believers spread his kingdom: a kingdom of truth and life, a kingdom of holiness and grace, a kingdom of justice, love and peace. In this kingdom creation itself will be set free from its slavery to corruption, to receive the freedom of the glory of the children of God . . . .**
>
> **Believers must learn the deepest meaning and the value of all creation, and how it leads to the praise of God.**
>
> **Believers must assist one another, even in their daily occupations to live holier lives. Then the world will be permeated with the Spirit of Christ and realise its goal of justice, love and peace.'**   *The Church*, no 36.

Space for your own notes

WALKING ON WATER

WALKING ON WATER is a programme of biblical instruction. It offers books and videos that mutually supplement each other, as input for personal study and/or group discussion.

WALKING ON WATER will eventually provide *seven courses*. Each *course book* contains information on the Gospel and notes for reflection. The accompanying *videos* present life stories about Christians in various parts of the world.

Courses in preparation:

1. **Gospel and Community.** Life stories from London, Sao Paolo and Brazil (release: April 1991).
2. **My Galilee, My People.** Life stories from Colombia (release: November 1990).
3. **The Gospel transcends barriers.** Life stories from Indonesia (release: November 1991).
4. **Religion of the Heart.** Life stories from Taiwan (release: February 1992).
5. **The Signs of the Kingdom.** Life stories from Zaire, Zimbabwe and South Africa (release: November 1992).
6. **God Comes Close.** Life stories from India (release: 1993).
7. **Resurrection.** Life stories from Europe (release: 1993).

For information, contact: Housetop, 39 Homer Street, London W1H 1HL. Tel. 071 - 402 9679.